This journal belongs to

....

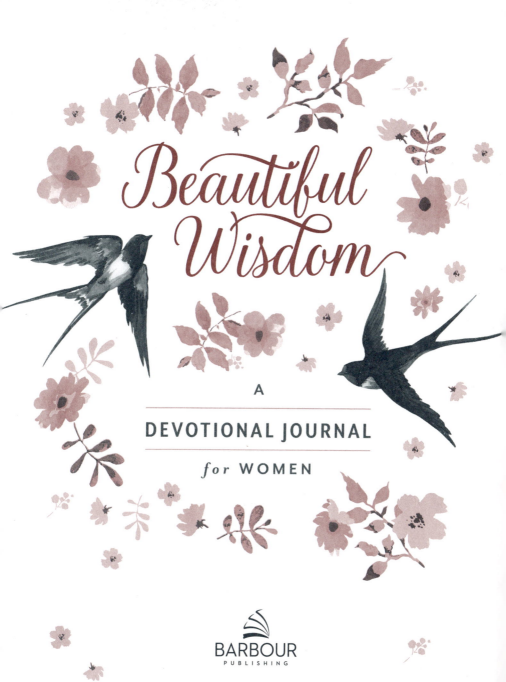

Beautiful Wisdom

A

DEVOTIONAL JOURNAL

for WOMEN

BARBOUR
PUBLISHING

© 2022 by Barbour Publishing, Inc.

ISBN 978-1-63609-336-9

Cover and Interior Design: Greg Jackson, Thinkpen Design

Published by Barbour Publishing, Inc., 1810 Barbour Drive, Uhrichsville, Ohio 44683, www.barbourbooks.com

Our mission is to inspire the world with the life-changing message of the Bible.

Printed in China.

For if a man belongs to Christ, he is a new person. The old life is gone. New life has begun.
2 Corinthians 5:17

God's Word is living and powerful and sharper than a sword (Hebrews 4:12), and through His Son, we have new life (Romans 6:4). This devotional collection will speak to your heart with scriptures carefully selected from the accessible, easy-to-understand New Life Bible. Spend quiet time immersed in the beautiful wisdom only the living and active Word of the Creator of the Universe can provide, and be blessed!

The Publisher

The Dream-Maker

"No eye has ever seen or no ear has ever heard or no mind has ever thought of the wonderful things God has made ready for those who love Him."

1 CORINTHIANS 2:9

Dreams, goals, and expectations are part of our daily lives. We have an idea of what we want and how we're going to achieve it. Disappointment can raise its ugly head when what we wanted—what we expected—doesn't happen like we thought it should or doesn't happen as fast as we planned.

Disappointment can lead to doubt. Perhaps questions tempt you to doubt the direction you felt God urging you to pursue. Don't quit! Don't give up! Press on with your dream. Failure isn't failure until you quit. When it looks like it's over, stand strong. With God's assistance, there is another way, a higher plan, or a better time to achieve your dream.

God knows the dreams He has placed inside of you. He created you and knows what you can do—even better than you know yourself. Maintain your focus—not on the dream but on the Dream Maker—and together you will achieve your dream.

God, thank You for putting dreams in my heart. I refuse to quit. I'm looking to You to show me how to reach my dreams. Amen.

Say What?

*Obey the Word of God. If you hear only and
do not act, you are only fooling yourself.*
JAMES 1:22

Have you ever been introduced to someone and immediately forgotten the person's name? Similarly, have you ever tried to talk to someone who is engrossed in a television show? "Yeah, I'm listening," the person replies in a less-than-attentive voice.

James seems to be in a similar situation. He is frustrated by those who pretend to listen and yet do not apply what they have heard. Like a person who sits through a speech and afterward cannot list the main points, so the people to whom James writes have heard the Word of God and cannot—or will not—apply it.

So often we find ourselves tuning out the minister on Sunday morning or thinking about other things as we read our Bibles or sing songs of praise. We look up at the end of a sermon, a stanza, a chapter, and we don't know what we've heard, sung, or read. We pretend to hear, but we are really letting the Word of God go in one ear and out the other. Our minds must be disciplined to really listen to God's Word. Then we must do the more difficult thing—*act* on what we've finally heard.

Dear Lord, please teach me to be attentive to Your
Word. Help me to act on the things You teach me
so that mine becomes a practical faith. Amen.

Disaster!

I will be safe in the shadow of Your wings until the trouble has passed.

PSALM 57:1

Natural disasters bring about a host of responses from people. Understandably, many individuals weep and mourn. Others look for the silver lining or even some humor in devastation. That was the response of Charlie Jones.

He found his office underwater. Records, machinery, data, personal items—all of it—ruined by flooding. He didn't cry. He didn't scream. He didn't curse. He said he did what most grown men in his situation would do.

He began to suck his thumb.

In that moment, he said later, he heard the voice of God.

"It's okay, Charlie. I was gonna burn it all anyway."

We find little good in the premature loss of things that harbor dear memories for us. But God's Word is filled with promises of renewal and restoration. We may not see it today or next month or even ten years from now. Nevertheless, our Lord's name is Redeemer. He alone can and will redeem the valuable, the precious, the everlastingly worthwhile.

If we find no comfort in the words God whispered to Charlie, we have a sure Word of God that we can hold on to in our tears. "He suffered with them in all their troubles" (Isaiah 63:9).

Lord, You are in control of all things. When I'm
overwhelmed with terrible events in my life, draw me
close to You for the help I so desperately need. Amen.

10

Created vs. Creator

"Be careful not to lift up your eyes toward heaven and see the sun and moon and stars, all the things of heaven, and be pulled away and worship them and serve them. The Lord your God has given these things to all the nations under the whole heavens."

DEUTERONOMY 4:19

The sun, moon, and stars are not to guide our lives, regardless of the power their light seems to have over us or the horoscopes people have concocted. God placed those lights in the sky with the touch of His little finger and could turn them off again, if He so chose, with less effort than it would take to flip a switch. They are beautiful creations, but they do not compare with the Creator!

Once in a while nature takes our breath away. We marvel at snowcapped mountains or get caught up in the colors of a sunset. Our heavenly Father is like a loving parent on Christmas Eve who arranges gifts beneath the tree, anticipating the joy those gifts will bring to his children.

When God fills the sky with a gorgeous sunset, it is not just about the colors and the beauty. Those colors reflect His love. He paints each stroke, each tiny detail, and mixes purples with pinks and yellows so that you might *look up*! When you look up to find the bright lights that govern our days and nights or the next time you see a sunset, remember the Creator and give Him glory.

Father, thank You for the beauty of Your world. Remind me to stand in awe of the Creator, not the created. Amen.

Spring

*There is a special time for everything. There is a
time for everything that happens under heaven.*

ECCLESIASTES 3:1

Don't you love the four seasons? They represent change, and change can
be a good thing. Springtime is delightful because it's filled with images
of new life. Rebirth. Joy. All you have to do is look around you and your
heart can come alive. Flowers budding. Trees blossoming. Dry, brown grass
morphing to green. This season is a true do-over, isn't it?!

The Bible teaches us that God ordained the seasons. He set them in
place and wants us to enjoy them. In the same way, we go through different "seasons" in our spiritual lives too. Think about it. Our hearts can get
frozen over (winter). Then God breathes new life into us and a thawing
begins (springtime). From there, we move into full blossom, a season of
productivity (summer). Then, as with all things, we slow down, preparing
for change (autumn).

Yes, God surely ordained the seasons, but springtime is one with a
remarkable sense of expectation, so enjoy it!

Father, I love springtime! Everything feels so new,
so fresh. I'm ready to put yesterday behind me. The
heaviness of the "winter" seasons in my life evaporates
on a warm breeze. I appreciate the lessons learned over
the past several months, but I'm so happy it's spring!

Eye Care

For the Lord of All says, "The Lord of shining-greatness has sent Me against the nations which have robbed you in battle. For whoever touches you, touches what is of great worth to Him."

ZECHARIAH 2:8

The apple of the eye refers to the pupil—the very center, or heart, of the eye. Consider the lengths we go to in order to protect our eyes. We wear protective glasses in some workplaces. We close our eyes or squint in windstorms or bright light. When dust blows, we turn our heads or put up our hands to keep the dirt from ending up in our eyes.

When we do get something in an eye, the ache and discomfort are instant. Tears form, and we seek to get the particle out as quickly as possible to stop the pain. If we are unable to remove the offending bit, we often become unable to do anything but focus on the discomfort.

To think that we are the apple of God's eye is incredible. Consider the care He must take for us. He will go to great lengths to protect us from harm. When something or someone does attack us, God feels our pain. He is instantly aware of our discomfort, for it is His own. When the storms of life come, we must remember how God feels each twinge of suffering. Despite the adversity, we can praise God for He is sheltering us.

Thank You, God, that You are so aware of what is happening to me. Thank You for Your protection. Amen.

Shut the Door

"When you pray, go into a room by yourself. After you have shut the door, pray to your Father Who is in secret. Then your Father Who sees in secret will reward you."

MATTHEW 6:6

We all have lists: things to buy, things to do, even a list for God. *Lord, I want. . .God, I need. . .and if You could please. . .*

He meets your needs because He loves you and wants to give you His best. Have you ever wondered what God wants? He wants you—your attention, affection, praise, and worship. He wants to be included in your life.

Prayer isn't just a time to give God our list but a time to enjoy each other's company, just as you would if you were to take time with a close personal friend—and that's really who He is. In the busyness of life, we must be careful that our "quiet time" never becomes insignificant because it's limited to the needs we feel we must tell God about. We must remember our most precious desire—just spending time with Him.

Find a moment today, shut out the rest of the world, and discover truly how little anything else matters but God. No one knows the path He's chosen for you quite like He does. Let Him point you to the truth and bring about the results He destined for you before the beginning of time.

Father, forgive me for not taking time to spend with You.
Help me to listen and include You in my life at all times. Amen.

He Is Faithful

If we have no faith, He will still be faithful
for He cannot go against what He is.

2 TIMOTHY 2:13

Have you ever said you'll do something, knowing full well you probably wouldn't get it done? We humans have a knack for letting each other down; deals fall through, plans crumble, agreements are breached.

Sometimes we treat our relationship with God the same as we do with other people. We promise Him we'll start spending more time with Him in prayer and Bible study. *This time, it will be different—I'll stick with it,* we think. Soon the daily distractions of life get in the way, and we're back in our same routine, minus prayer and Bible study.

Even when we fail to live up to our expectations, our heavenly Father doesn't pick up His judge's gavel and condemn us for unfaithfulness. Instead, He remains a faithful supporter, encouraging us to keep trying to hold up our end of the bargain. Take comfort in His faithfulness, and let that encourage you toward a deeper relationship with Him.

Father, thank You for Your unending faithfulness. Every day I fall short of Your standards, but You're always there, encouraging me and lifting me up. Please help me to be more faithful to You—in the big things and in the little things. Amen.

Joy in the Ride

Many flowers will grow in it, and it will be filled with joy and singing.

ISAIAH 35:2

What if we viewed life as an adventurous bicycle ride? With our destination in focus, we would pedal forward but not so swiftly as to overlook the beauty and experiences that God planted along the way.

We would note the tenacity of a wildflower in bloom despite its unlikely location for growth. We would contemplate God's mercy and savor the brilliance of a rainbow that illuminated a once-blackened sky.

At our halfway point, we would relax from the journey, finding a spot in life's shade to refresh and replenish ourselves for the return trip. We wouldn't just live; we would explore, pausing along the way to inhale the fresh air and scent of wildflowers.

In life, however, sometimes the road gets rough, and we are forced to take sharp turns. When that happens, we miss the beauty that surrounds us. But if we savor the ride and keep moving forward despite the bumps in the road, then "joy and singing" will follow.

So when your legs grow weary and your pathway seems long, brace yourself, board your bike, and keep on pedaling. Joy awaits you just around the bend.

Oh Lord, pave my pathway with song, even when the road is rough. Remind me to stop and appreciate the scenery along the way. Only then will I experience the joy awaiting me. Amen.

Seek First

"First of all, look for the holy nation of God. Be right with Him. All these other things will be given to you also."

MATTHEW 6:33

What do you seek? Wealth, harmonious relationships, an impressive home, power, a devoted spouse, a fulfilling career? The list can go on and on. We spend much time, energy, and resources chasing after what we think our hearts desire. Yet when we get what we want, are we truly content? Or do we simply pause until another tempting carrot is dangled before us?

Our Creator knows where we will find true contentment. Seeking the things of this world will never be enough. Our hearts yearn for more. Our souls search for everlasting love and inner joy. God meets our need in the person of Jesus Christ. If we attempt to fill the emptiness of our soul with anything or anyone else, it's like chasing after the wind. We will come up empty-handed and disillusioned.

Seeking His kingdom begins by entering into a relationship with our heavenly Father through the person of Jesus Christ. Accept Jesus as your Savior. Then honor Him as Lord in your daily life. Focus on God's priorities. Value people above possessions, eternal riches over earthly ones. When we seek first His kingdom and righteousness, we have obtained the most treasured possession. He will take care of the rest.

Dear Lord, may I have the desire to seek
You above everything else. Amen.

Build for Today

"Build houses and live in them. Plant gardens and eat their fruit."
JEREMIAH 29:5

Skeptics sometimes accuse Christians of being so heavenly minded that they are no earthly good. Today few of us would sell all our earthly possessions and camp out on a hilltop, waiting for the Lord's return. However, we still often live in "Tomorrowland."

Tomorrow, we think, *we will serve God more fully, after our children are grown and we have more time. Tomorrow we will give more, after we have paid off the car and saved enough for a down payment on a house. Tomorrow we will study the Bible more, after we no longer work full-time.*

Jeremiah's audience, Jews deported from their homeland to Babylon, knew all about Tomorrowland. They said, "Soon God will return us to our homes. As soon as that happens, we will serve God." They lived with their suitcases packed, ready to return.

God sent a stern message through His prophet Jeremiah. "You're going to be there a long time. Put down roots where I have sent you."

God sends the same message to us. He wants us to live for today. We can't allow dreams for tomorrow to paralyze our lives today.

God's presence enables us to live in the present.

Dear Heavenly Father, You have given us the gift of today. You want us to plant gardens and make homes. Show us joy and fulfillment in the present. Amen.

Infinite and Personal

*"Am I a God Who is near," says the Lord, "and not a God
Who is far away? . . . Do I not fill heaven and earth?"*

Back in the 1950s, the Union of Soviet Socialist Republics sent up its first satellite, *Sputnik*. At that time, Communism held Russia in its tightfisted grip. Everyone who was anyone in the USSR was a Communist and an atheist. Not long after *Sputnik*, the Russian cosmonauts circled planet Earth. After their return, one cosmonaut made this announcement to the world: "I saw no God anywhere."

When U.S. astronauts finally made it into space some months later, one remarked, "I saw God everywhere!"

Our worldview determines the way we see reality. The cosmonaut didn't expect to see God, and he didn't. The astronaut didn't see anything more or less than his Russian counterpart, but he came away with an entirely different response. God says that He is both close at hand and over all there is. The late theologian and philosopher Francis Schaeffer called Him the infinite-personal God.

Whether your day is crumbling around you or it is the best day you have ever had, do you see God in it? If the "sky is falling" or the sun is shining, do you still recognize the One who orders all the planets and all your days? Whether we see Him or not, God tells us He is there. And He's here too—in the good times and bad.

Lord, empower me to trust You when it's hard to
remember that You are near. And help me to live
thankfully when times are good. Amen.

Busy Waiting

"Not one of these men of these sinful people will see the good land I promised to give your fathers."

DEUTERONOMY 1:35

For forty years, those woeful Israelites wandered through the desert to reach the Promised Land. How often they must have stared down at a valley or looked to the mountain summits, dreading the thousands of steps required to get there. Scholars have determined that forty-year journey should have taken only three days—at the very most, two weeks.

Imagine the mechanics of moving more than two million people through the desert. They must have had an organized method for moving so many bodies. Each person probably had duties and responsibilities. Their wandering existence must have become normal, even routine.

But that generation of Israelites had no real purpose to their lives. They were busy people but faithless. No Bible verses applaud their lives. It's as if they never lived at all. Despite witnessing miracle after miracle, they never saw those tests as opportunities to trust God in a deeper way. What wasted lives!

And what a lesson to the rest of us! Are we trusting and depending on God in deeper ways throughout our full and busy days? Or are we merely moving from one spot to the next, productive but not purposeful—busy waiting?

Lord, I don't want to wander aimlessly, unaware of how
purposeless my life is. I want my life to count! With single-
hearted devotion, may I look to You in all things. Amen.

Pleasing God

His joy is not in the strength of a horse. He does not find
joy in the legs of a man. But the Lord favors those who fear
Him and those who wait for His loving-kindness.

PSALM 147:10–11

Americans value achievement. We measure our country by its various accomplishments. Scientific discovery, space exploration, technological advancement, and world economic and political power all attest to the hard work and achievement of people building a nation.

As individuals, we measure our days by how much we get done. We take pride in checking items off our to-do lists. We email on our handheld devices while sitting in airports and talk on our phones while driving down the highway in an effort to maximize our time so we can get more accomplished in a day.

God does not place value on our achievements. He does not measure our days by how much we get done. He is not delighted by our efficiency or our excellence. This is pretty hard to believe because our culture places such value on self-reliance, but what pleases Him is our worship of Him. He wants our reverent fear, our wonder and awe at His great power and steadfast love. He desires our dependence. He enjoys our hope when we are looking to Him to meet all our needs.

Great God, who gave Your Son for all my sins, help
me to remember that I do not have to perform for
You. You have redeemed me and made me Your own.
You desire my worship and my hope. Amen.

Add Love

And to all these things, you must add love. Love holds everything and everybody together and makes all these good things perfect.
COLOSSIANS 3:14

Paul wrote a letter to the Colossians, a church he loved and had spent time with, a group of people whom he knew needed this advice. We need the same advice today. He told the Colossians that as God's people, they were dearly loved. He admonished them to exhibit compassion, kindness, and humility. As if this was not enough, Paul also told them to show gentleness and to have patience with one another. He told them to bear with one another and to forgive one another as the Lord had forgiven them. Then Paul said a peculiar thing, but it really makes a lot of sense. He told them to *put on love.*

But how does one "wear" love? Imagine a winter morning. You put on long underwear, then a shirt, followed by a sweater, and on top of all that, you wear a coat. It binds it all together. Like the bun on a burger! Like the chocolate wafers of an ice cream sandwich! What enables you to forgive, to show compassion, to be gentle? What can cause even the most type-A personality to be patient with another believer? Love. Only love. It binds it all together. It causes the Christian to look and act and even feel different from the non-Christian. It is the greatest of all the virtues. Don't start your day without putting on love!

Father, let Your love show in all that I do today. Help me to be quick to forgive others as You have forgiven me. Amen.

Heavenly Treasure

"Gather together riches in heaven where they will not be eaten by bugs or become rusted. Men cannot break in and steal them."

MATTHEW 6:20

You've got ten minutes to leave your home before it is destroyed by fire. What will you take with you? Once you knew your loved ones were safe, you would likely grab the things that remind you of them—photos, heirloom jewelry, a precious family Bible.

Questions like these have a way of whittling our priorities down to the bare essentials. Most of what we own is easily destroyed and just as easily replaced. There are, however, a few things really worth having, and Jesus reminds us that these are things on which we can't put a price tag. Relationships. Eternal life. The assurance that our loved ones will live eternally with Him.

What will you take with you? This isn't a rhetorical question. The practicality of Jesus' words reminds us that the way we live our lives each and every day should be guided by this principle. Invest yourself in the things that matter. Take a look at your calendar and your checkbook. Do they reflect your desire to store up eternal treasures?

Lord, You know it is easy to get distracted by earthly things—
things that will ultimately be worth nothing. Help me to shift
my focus to matters that have eternal significance, and help me to
invest my life in those things that will bring eternal dividends.

Who's in Control?

At the right time, we will be shown that God is the One Who has all power. He is the King of kings and Lord of lords.

1 TIMOTHY 6:15

Hannah was having second thoughts about her visit to Italy as a short-term missionary. Between the language challenges and cultural taboos, her jet-lagged brain was in overdrive. Things continued to worsen with each passing day.

On her second trip to the bureau where she had to finalize some legal papers for her stay, she stood in the pouring rain to keep her place in line. Like everyone else, Hannah stood in two inches of water. Once inside, the situation wasn't much better. The person she had to speak to wasn't there. He couldn't make it in; his car was under three feet of water. Hannah would have to make a third trip back. Disgruntled, she and her host left.

The street had become a lake. People were walking in thigh-high water. Everyone was trying to walk, wade, or swim their way to their cars and go home. Hannah and her host saw one man who wasn't about to let the flooding best him. He walked down the street clothed in his T-shirt and underwear, holding his pants above the garbage-strewn street river.

Hannah looked for a sign that read, Welcome to your mission field.

Sometimes when we go on what we're sure is a God-ordained mission, bad things happen. In spite of inconveniences over which we've no control, we can rest in knowing God retains control. Some days we just have to trudge our way through—and look for a laugh along the way.

In my frustrations, Father, remind me that You're in control. Amen.

Using Time Wisely

So be careful how you live. Live as men who are wise and not
foolish. Make the best use of your time. These are sinful days.
Ephesians 5:15–16

Is your testimony something you review on a regular basis? It should be.
This world is full of darkness, and God needs dedicated Christians who
truly love Him to shed His light on lost souls.

Our primary desire should be to bring people to Jesus. This doesn't
mean that all we ever do is talk about God, but when He gives us opportunities, we should take them. No matter what we are doing or saying, it
should always honor God.

Our time on earth is limited, and we must use every minute wisely. We
will give an account of all our time, whether we waste it or use it for God's
glory. That is why it is so important to look often at how we measure up
to God's expectations for our lives.

Jesus is our ideal. It really doesn't matter if we are better or worse than
someone else. If we don't measure up to Christ, there is work to be done.
We must let God work in and through us that we might wisely use the
time He gives us to make a difference for Him.

O God, give me a desire to make every moment I have
count for You. Help me be wise in how I conduct my life.

Keep Short Accounts

*"He that is faithful with little things is faithful with big
things also. He that is not honest with little things is not
honest with big things. If you have not been faithful with
riches of this world, who will trust you with true riches?"*

LUKE 16:10–11

Credit cards seem like such a simple and easy way to buy all we want.
Sometimes, though, plastic helps us acquire not only a bunch of stuff but
a mountain of debt as well. Good intentions can result in never-ending
bills, interest charges, and minimum payments that barely chip away at
the actual money owed. Buying on credit allows us to immediately fulfill
our desires for things we want, but this isn't God's way. Instead, He desires
us to be wise in our wealth.

When we prove to be faithful with our own finances, God will trust
us with the bigger things in life. If we patiently wait for the blessings of
life to come, we will reap the rewards of satisfaction, financial security, and
the trust of others. Exercise godly principles by making sound financial
decisions and faithfully honoring the gifts God gives.

Jesus, thank You for the rich blessings in my life. Please help me to
be patient and wise with my finances. I want to be faithful with the
little things so that I will be worthy of trust in the big ones. Amen.

Honor God with Healthy Habits

So honor God with your body.
1 CORINTHIANS 6:20

The statistics are grim. More than half of Americans are overweight or obese. Only about a third of us get the minimum recommended amount of exercise each day. Health problems that were once reserved for elderly people—like diabetes and high blood pressure—are now affecting us at younger and younger ages.

In spite of living in a society obsessed with diet and exercise, many of us are becoming more unhealthy. Yet the Bible says to honor God with our bodies. We often think of this verse in relation to sexual purity, and it certainly applies. However, we also have an opportunity to honor God with our bodies by taking good care of them—by getting enough rest and enough exercise.

Take a look in the mirror. You need at least eight hours of sleep each night so your body can function optimally. Do you make it a priority to get enough rest, or do you stretch yourself to the limit all week, then try to make up for it on the weekends? Adults should get 30 to 60 minutes of physical activity most days of the week. Is there time in your day for fresh air and exercise, or do you spend long hours sitting at a desk in a stuffy building? It sounds like a cliché, but you only get one body—make it a priority to honor God with it.

Father, thank You for blessing me with a body that does
so much for me. Please help me to make it a priority
to care for it in a way that honors You. Amen.

Unswerving Faith

Let us hold on to the hope we say we have and not be changed.
We can trust God that He will do what He promised.

HEBREWS 10:23

Do you remember your first bicycle? Maybe it was a hand-me-down from an older sibling or one found at a neighborhood garage sale. Or maybe you remember the joy of discovering a brand-new bike on Christmas morning. In your delight, you never wondered how Santa got it down the chimney!

Do you remember learning to ride your bike? What a process! While mastering putting it all together—the pedaling, the steering, the balance—did you ever lose control? When you started to swerve, it was a lost cause. Regaining momentum was practically impossible. Almost inevitably, the bike tipped over, and you ended up in the grass.

"Keep it straight!" parents call out when they see their child headed for yet another bike crash. "Look where you're going! Hold it steady!" Similarly, the author of Hebrews challenges us to hold *unswervingly* to our hope in Christ Jesus. Certainly, we fail to do this at times, but life is much better when we keep our eyes fixed on Him.

Sometimes just a whisper from Satan, the father of lies, can cause shakiness where once there was steadfastness. Place your hope in Christ alone. He will help you resist the lies of this world. Hold *unswervingly* to your Savior today. He is faithful!

Jesus, You are the object of my hope. There are many distractions in my life, but I pray that You will help me keep my eyes on You. Thank You for Your faithfulness. Amen.

Go with God

"Go and make followers of all the nations. Baptize them
in the name of the Father and of the Son and of the Holy
Spirit. Teach them to do all the things I have told you.
And I am with you always, even to the end of the world."

MATTHEW 28:19–20

Have you ever had to make a presentation? Maybe you had the opportunity to teach a class at your workplace or church. Wasn't it a boost to have a coworker or friend there for moral support? Even if that person just nodded occasionally in the audience, assisted with passing out papers, or adjusted the laptop or projector for you, it was a blessing to not go it alone.

Having the moral support of a friend is great, but the promise of the Great Commission scriptures is even greater. The God of the universe gives believers a command in these verses, but He does not tell us to go and teach the Gospel on our own. He makes His intention very clear: He promises to be with us always.

Ask God to reveal to you the people in your life who need to hear the good news of Jesus. As He shows you lost friends and family members, share the Gospel through word and deed and claim God's promise to be with you.

Father, thank You for the joy of sharing Christ with
others. Remind me that You accompany me as I follow
Your command to go and make disciples. Amen.

The Open Door

"For everyone who asks, will receive what he asks for.
Everyone who looks, will find what he is looking for.
Everyone who knocks, will have the door opened to him."

LUKE 11:10

The whole process of looking for a job can be overwhelming—not just the first time but every time. From preparing and sending out your résumé to the interviews, the fear of the unknown can weigh heavily on you. If only someone would just give you a chance to show what you can do.

You don't have to be a bundle of nerves. You can rest assured that God has prepared a place for you. He has the right environment for you to flourish and grow in, as well as people in that environment who need what you have to offer to help the company succeed.

Be confident in who He created you to be. Trust Him to place you in the right place. You do your best, and He'll do His part. Ask Him for direction and guidance to lead you to the right people, places, and choices. Don't become discouraged if what you want and what He wants for you are a little different. He perfects everything that concerns you. Place yourself in His capable hands.

Heavenly Father, please open the door to that fulfilling job that You've created just for me, one that will meet all my needs. Direct me to the right place, and give me wisdom and favor. I'm trusting You! Amen.

50

Display His Glory

We have this light from God in our human bodies. This shows
that the power is from God. It is not from ourselves.

2 CORINTHIANS 4:7

Many Christians struggle with the fact that they struggle. We forget our frailty. We don't remember that our spiritual growth is as much a work of Christ as our salvation. We find ourselves frustrated and disappointed because we fail to live up to our own high expectations of ourselves.

At the root of this thought pattern is our pride. We are trying to live out our faith in our own strength—but we can't. We forget that the Bible says we are clay pots. Our Father deliberately places the treasure of knowing Christ into a jar of clay.

Think of bright red geraniums filling clay pots in summer or an exquisite orchid planted in an ordinary clay pot. Picture fuchsia blooms, waxy green leaves, and soft petals that stand in contrast to the rough pot that contains the plant. Drop the clay pot on the patio, and it will break. Leave it out in extreme cold, and it will crack. Place it in a wet, shady spot, and moss will grow on its sides. The pot alone is not valuable, strong, or beautiful, but when filled with blossoms, it becomes a joy to behold.

Father, help me not to think too highly of myself. Help
me to remember that I am made of dust but that You have
placed the treasure of Your Son in me to display His glory.

The Same in a Changing World

The grass dries up. The flower loses its color.
But the Word of our God stands forever.

ISAIAH 40:8

The world has changed so much in the past one hundred years. Electricity, indoor plumbing, airplanes and automobiles, computers, smartphones, GPS, and countless other technologies have created an entirely new world. Perhaps you have flipped through a yellowed photo album with pictures of your great-great-grandparents and then looked at perfectly preserved digital photos on a computer. Or maybe you remember a day when you paid much less for that gallon of gas or cup of coffee than you did yesterday morning. The world is changing, but our God is not.

God is the constant in our lives. His Word was, is, and will always be the same. It's amazing to think that while we cannot imagine life without electricity, someone hundreds of years ago read the same Bible we read and was learning to trust in God just as we are learning to trust in Him. God's Word is for all people, regardless of the world they live in. God speaks to His people no matter where they are in life. Hundreds of years before the birth of Christ, Isaiah proclaimed that the Word of our God stands forever. Praise be to the Lord that we are still able to proclaim that same message today!

Dear Lord, thank You for Your unchanging Word. Thank You for Your love and for the comfort of knowing that You are the same yesterday, today, and forever. Amen.

God Cares about Your Disappointments

You have seen how many places I have gone. Put my
tears in Your bottle. Are they not in Your book?
PSALM 56:8

There are disappointments in the Christian life. God has not promised us otherwise. When sin entered the world in the garden that day through a bite of fruit, disappointment was instantly included in the consequences. This is a fallen world. We live and move and have our being in a place that truly is not our home. One day and for all eternity, in heaven, everything will be perfect as it is supposed to be. We will spend our days praising God. There will be no more tears or loss. We will not be let down or hurt in any way. But here, and for now, there is disappointment. We must learn to live with it. We should embrace it even.

It is in the sorrows of life that God shows Himself so real and loving. He is near to the brokenhearted. The Bible says He "collects our tears." Have you gone through a divorce that you never dreamed would take place? Are you heartbroken over a child's decisions? Has someone hurt you or abandoned you at the time you needed him or her most? God is there in the midst of the hurt. He may not always take the storm away, but He will always ride it out with you. Take refuge in the Lord. He cares for you.

Thank You, heavenly Father, for caring when
I hurt. Even in my disappointments, I can see
You at work in my life. I love You, Lord. Amen.

Christ Is Involved

*I am sure that God Who began the good work in you will keep
on working in you until the day Jesus Christ comes again.*
PHILIPPIANS 1:6

When you accepted Jesus as Savior, that was just the beginning of His work in your life. Yes, salvation was complete through His grace. Your sins were forgiven, and your home in heaven was secured.

But Christ wants so much more for you. He wants you to grow in your faith. He wants to help you flee the temptations that you will inevitably face. He wants to give you strength to be joyful even as you go through trials. His ultimate desire is to help you become more like Him.

Do you allow Jesus to be as involved in your life as He wants to be? Unfortunately, a lot of people accept Him in order to get into heaven, but then they want little more to do with Him. Why not choose now to let Him be a part of everything you do and every decision you make? Go to Him in prayer. Seek answers from His Word and from the Holy Spirit. He will do a great work in your life. He will be faithful to complete what He started in you—and you will become like Him.

Dear Jesus, thank You for wanting to help me be
like You. Thank You for being involved in my life
and not leaving me to my own designs.

When You Are Tempted

You have never been tempted to sin in any different way than other people. God is faithful. He will not allow you to be tempted more than you can take. But when you are tempted, He will make a way for you to keep from falling into sin.

1 Corinthians 10:13

Have you ever felt that temptation was just too great? Have you given in to it? You are not alone. It is not easy to resist temptation. Satan, the prince of darkness, is always seeking to devour God's children. He knows your personal weaknesses and uses them against you. The good news is that there is always a way out when you are tempted to sin. Every temptation that you have ever faced or will face in the future has been experienced by others. No temptation is new. Satan just recycles the same juicy bait and uses it again and again, generation after generation. Staying in God's Word and praying daily will help you to resist temptation. Being part of a Christian community will help with this also. As you bring down your walls and allow other believers to get close to you, they can pray for you and hold you accountable. Remember that no matter what temptations you are facing today, the pay-off will be far greater if you resist than if you give in. Jesus stands ready to help you escape if only you will reach out and take His hand.

Lord, help me in this area today: (fill in this blank with your area of greatest temptation to sin). I need to see the way out. Thank You, Father. Amen.

Happy in Hope

Be happy in your hope. Do not give up when trouble comes. Do not let anything stop you from praying.

ROMANS 12:12

Romans 12:12 tells believers to be joyful in hope, patient, and faithful. This is a tall order. The good news is that believers can be strong even in weakness because of Christ living in us. We can do all things through Him—including being hopeful, patient, and faithful in prayer.

Hope is sometimes described as "the present enjoyment of a future blessing." Even if your situation is difficult now and doesn't improve while you are on earth, you are promised eternity with Him. He will make all things right in His time.

Patience is a virtue we teasingly warn each other never to pray for! Throughout our lives, we face trials both small and great. Whether your affliction is sitting in traffic or a cancer diagnosis, seek to be patient. Wait upon the Lord. Rest in Him, trust that He is in control, and lay your anxiety at the feet of your Savior.

Faithfulness in prayer requires discipline. God is faithful regardless of our attitude toward Him. He never changes, wavers, or forsakes His own. We may be faithful to do daily tasks around the house. We feed the cat, wash the clothes, and empty the trash. But faithfulness in the quiet discipline of prayer is harder. There are seemingly no consequences for neglecting our time with the Lord. Oh, what a myth this is! Set aside a daily time for prayer, and see how the Lord blesses you, transforming your spirit to increase your joyful hope, your patience, and your faithfulness.

Faithful God, find me faithful. Stir up the hope and joy within me. Give me the grace I need to wait on You. Amen.

Forgiving Others

He has taken our sins from us as far as the east is from the west.

PSALM 103:12

Forgiveness. The word rolls off the tongue much more easily than it penetrates the heart. When someone has wronged you, it is natural to feel hurt. It is not easy to forgive a person who has wounded you. Forgiveness is no small thing. It is a tall order. The greater the offense, the harder you may find it to forgive. The model prayer that Jesus taught His followers includes this line: *"Forgive us our trespasses as we forgive those who trespass against us."* What was Jesus saying here? He was reminding us to emulate our Father's ability to forgive. Have we not all sinned and fallen short of the glory of God? Certainly! But our heavenly Father forgives us. He removes the dark stain of sin and says He will speak of it no more. It is gone. As far as the east is from the west. That is a long way! God does not keep bringing up your past sins. If you have asked Him to forgive you, He has. Pray for your heavenly Father to reveal to you just how much He loves you. As you experience His love and forgiveness, you will want to forgive others—regardless of the depth of the hurt they have caused in your life.

God, forgiveness is not always easy. Help me to sense Your deep love for me. Remind me of all that You have forgiven me of so that I might be able to forgive others. Amen.

How to Please God

*"O my God, I know that You test the heart
and are pleased with what is right."*

1 Chronicles 29:17

Of all the character traits we look for in a friend, a potential mate, a leader, and especially an auto mechanic, integrity sits at the top of the list. King David was a man of integrity (1 Kings 9:4). Even Jesus' sharpest critics said, "We know You are true" (Mark 12:14). Paul encourages teachers to "show them how to live by your life and by right teaching. You should be wise in what you say. Then the one who is against you will be ashamed and will not be able to say anything bad about you" (Titus 2:7–8).

Not everyone, however, appreciates the honesty that characterizes the person of integrity. Proverbs tells us that "men who kill hate him without blame" (29:10).

Even though we don't know a lot about Hanani in the book of Nehemiah, one thing we're told is that "he was a faithful man and honored God with fear more than many" (Nehemiah 7:2). What a high compliment! To have that said of us prepares us for whatever challenges come our way. Whether we're given a pat on the back—or a push out the door—for our personal integrity, we can be confident that our integrity pleases God.

Lord, make me a person of integrity so that I never bring
shame to Your name or pain to Your heart. Amen.

Reflecting God in Our Work

Whatever work you do, do it with all your heart.
Do it for the Lord and not for men.
COLOSSIANS 3:23

Parents often tell their children to do their best in school or to behave well when they visit friends' homes. Children are a reflection of their parents. When a mom and dad send their offspring out into the world, they can only hope that the reflection will be a positive one.

As believers, we are God's children. No one is perfect, and for this there is grace. However, we may be the only reflection of our heavenly Father that some will ever see. Our attitudes and actions on the job speak volumes to those around us. Although it may be tempting to do just enough to get by, we put forth our best effort when we remember we represent God to the world. A Christian's character on the job should be a positive reflection of the Lord.

This is true of our work at home as well. No one would disagree that daily chores are often monotonous, but we are called to face them with a cheerful spirit. God will give us the ability to do so when we ask Him.

Father, help me today to represent You well through my
work. I want to reflect Your love in all I do. Amen.

Times of Trouble

You have turned my crying into dancing. You have taken
off my clothes made from hair, and dressed me with joy.
So my soul may sing praise to You, and not be quiet.
O Lord my God, I will give thanks to You forever.

PSALM 30:11–12

David knew times of trouble, and he also knew what it meant to be relieved of trouble. He experienced want and he experienced abundance. He hid in fear of losing his life to a king that he knew hated him. . .and later, he danced with joy, praising God, amazed at God's provision and protection. Can you relate? You probably have never been chased by a king and his armies. But every life is full of ups and downs. There will be times when all you can hope to do is survive in the shelter of the Lord's wing. You know He is there, but you cannot sense His presence. You trust Him, but you don't know how in the world He will turn things around. Just keep trusting. Just keep believing. Just keep praying. David cried out to the Lord for mercy. Not just this psalm but many others are filled with David's pleas to the Lord. God is faithful to hear our prayers. Just as He turned David's sorrow into joy, He can do the same for you.

Father, I ask You to turn my weeping into laughter. Teach
me to praise You no matter my circumstances. Amen.

Faultless

There is One Who can keep you from falling and can bring you before Himself free from all sin. He can give you great joy as you stand before Him in His shining-greatness.

JUDE 1:24

Who is at fault? Who is to blame? When something goes wrong at work, at home, or at church, someone is held accountable. People want to know who is responsible, who made a mistake. The ones pointing fingers of accusation don't always care about the truth as much as they do about making sure they aren't blamed for the transgression.

Ever since God confronted Adam and Eve in the Garden of Eden, we have been pointing fingers at someone else instead of taking responsibility for our own actions. Shame and fear make us want to deny we have done any wrong even when we have done so accidentally or by mistake. We value what God and other people think of us. When we are at odds with God or others over a transgression, we often become depressed.

Jesus loves us so much despite our shortcomings. He is the One who can keep us from falling—who can present us faultless before the Father. Because of this, we can have our joy restored no matter what. Whether we have done wrong and denied it or have been falsely accused, we can come into His presence to be restored and lifted up. Let us keep our eyes on Him instead of on our need to justify ourselves to God or others.

Thank You, Jesus, for Your cleansing love and for the joy we can find in Your presence. Amen.

An Unexpected Turn

"He has made my way safe."

2 SAMUEL 22:33

We always want to be in the right place at the right time. Life moves in a hurry, and with it, we thrust ourselves forward into each appointment or commitment. We get frustrated when we miss a turn or mistakenly veer down a wrong road.

What if you were to choose to put a different spin on the frustration of going out of your way? You can get bent out of shape and become frustrated because of the time you feel you have lost, or you can choose to believe that God makes your way perfect and He has kept you from harm's way. What if that wrong turn that you thought cost you ten extra minutes in traffic actually kept you from a fender-bender or something worse?

Instead of feeling lost and undone, consider that perhaps this was the path you were destined to take. A series of unfortunate events or a trip down an unexpected path can lead to a positive spin on your day. Be open to taking a different route today. It could open new doors of opportunity in unexpected ways.

Father, help me to relax, trusting that You order my
steps and make my way perfect every day. Amen.

What's in a Name?

Live your lives as the Good News of Christ says you should.
PHILIPPIANS 1:27

Many families take pride in their family name. A name that has been around for a long time often commands respect; perhaps it is associated with money, power, or fine workmanship. When someone from the family enters the community, he often is expected to be careful to represent his family name well, behaving with dignity and honor, or he runs the risk of sullying the family name. In the same way, an employee must act in a manner that reflects well upon her boss or her company, or she risks damaging the reputation of the entire firm.

As Christians, we are called to conduct ourselves in a manner worthy of the Gospel. We must uphold the name of Christ while accurately representing the Gospel. Just like employees who lose their temper and reflect badly on their company, when we succumb to sin, we may tear down the Gospel we work so hard to advocate. Our conduct, no matter the situation, should worthily reflect the Gospel of Christ.

Dear Lord, thank You for Your Word. Please
help me to conduct myself in a worthy manner.
Let my life be a reflection of You. Amen.

Enter through the Narrow Gate

"Go in through the narrow door. The door is wide and the road is easy that leads to hell. Many people are going through that door. But the door is narrow and the road is hard that leads to life that lasts forever. Few people are finding it."

MATTHEW 7:13–14

Although peer pressure is often associated with teenagers, adults also have to deal with this phenomenon. Human beings instinctively embrace a mob mentality. Following the crowd comes easy. Acceptance by others is important. From wearing the latest fashions to watching the most popular TV shows, we hate being viewed as weird. We'd rather blend in with those around us by getting lost in the crowd.

Jesus warns us that the crowd is traveling the road that leads to destruction. Paul describes the masses in Philippians 3:19 by saying, "Their god is their stomach. They take pride in things they should be ashamed of. All they think about are the things of this world." Believers are challenged to focus on the eternal—on things that have spiritual value. A choice is before us: embrace worldly values or adopt God's truth.

Dare to enter through the narrow gate for it is through the narrow gate that true life is found. Embrace the life that God has for you by choosing the road less traveled.

Dear Lord, give me courage to enter through the narrow gate and experience life as You intended. Amen.

The Lord's Loving-Kindness

O Lord, let Your loving-kindness be upon
us as we put our hope in You.

PSALM 33:22

We hope that our sports team will win the big game and that Starbucks will bring back its hazelnut macchiato. We also hope that our jobs will continue to fulfill us and pay our bills and that God will answer a heartfelt prayer with a long-awaited yes.

Whatever we're hoping for, it's easy to think that God doesn't care about the details of our lives. However, just as a parent cares about everything that happens to her child, so God longs to share every part of our day. Why not talk to Him about all our needs and desires?

As we sip our morning coffee, we can jot down thanks for morning blessings such as flavored creamers and hot water for our shower. While we do our jobs, we can regularly bring our concerns (and coworkers) before God's throne. We could keep scriptures scribbled on Post-it notes in our cubicle—or on our desk—to remind us to think with God's thoughts throughout the day instead of falling back on worldly patterns. When we lay our head on the pillow at night, we can voice the answered prayers that grace our lives, drifting off to sleep in gratitude at God's unfailing love.

Those small, simple actions add up to a day filled with hope and gratitude. . .and those days add up to a life well-lived.

Father God, thank You for Your unfailing love. Thinking on that love, which I haven't earned and can't repay, causes me to fall to my knees in hope, gratitude, and joy.

Jumping Hurdles

As for God, His way is perfect. The Word
of the Lord has stood the test.

PSALM 18:30

Sandy Allen prayed to be like the other girls, but she knew she never would. Throughout her childhood, she was ridiculed for her size and appearance. At over seven feet seven inches tall, Sandy holds the world record as the tallest living woman. She learned to confront adversity and accept her place in life. And with much determination, she learned to overcome the major obstacles she faced.

Obstacles appear in your path every day. The enemy of your soul wants to keep you from fulfilling your purpose and achieving your dream. You don't have to face challenges alone; you can depend on God to help you make it over the hurdles—tough decisions, physical pain, or financial insecurity.

Maybe there are times when you just don't think you can take one more disappointment or hurt. That's the perfect time to draw strength from God and His Word. Meditate on encouraging scriptures, or play a song that you know strengthens your heart and mind. Ask God to infuse you with His strength, and you'll find the power to take another step and another—until you find yourself on the other side of that challenge you're facing today.

God, give me strength each day to face the
obstacles I am to overcome. I am thankful that
I don't have to face them alone. Amen.

A Covering of Faith

Most important of all, you need a covering of faith in front of you. This is to put out the fire-arrows of the devil.
EPHESIANS 6:16

When Paul wrote to the church at Ephesus about the shield of faith, he used the word *thureos*, which means "door." Roman soldiers' shields were large, rectangular, and door-sized. In other words, they covered every single part of the soldier's body. It's the same with our faith. The salvation we've been given in Christ covers us from head to toe. And because He is lavish in love and steadfast in keeping His promises, we'll always have enough for every situation we encounter.

The Roman soldiers' shields had one other distinctive quality: they were made of several hides of leather sewn together. This meant that every morning, a soldier would have to rub oil into the shield in order to keep it pliable and to prevent it from drying out and cracking. This daily renewal was the difference between life and death. . .literally!

In our own faith-walk, we must daily allow God's Holy Spirit to refill and re-energize us. The Spirit replenishes our joy, rebuilds our faith, and redirects our thoughts so that we can live boldly and courageously for Jesus. This begs the question: What have we done today to oil our shields? Let's not get complacent and allow distractions to deter us from our duty! In Christ, we have a true shield that won't ever let us down. Praise the Lord!

Lord, thank You for Your Word and all the riches I find there.
Give me the discipline to come to You regularly for refilling.

God Will Not Change

*"For I, the Lord, do not change. So you,
O children of Jacob, are not destroyed."*

Malachi 3:6

Perhaps one of the most important truths that we need to recognize is that God doesn't change. Often we are guilty of trying to bring God down to our level so we can be comfortable in our worldly standards.

"God understands that society changes," we say. "If we are going to reach today's people, we must incorporate some of their behaviors."

Yes, God knows that society changes, and what is sad is that His people change right along with it. God, however, does not change. His standards for purity, friendship, entertainment—and the list goes on—are the same that He established from the beginning. It is true that He wants us to reach those around us, but His power is great enough that He can help us do so through godly behavior. Unfortunately, it is more often our desire to fit in than a true desire to win others that causes us to adopt the world's standards.

It is time for us to acknowledge that God remains the same. We must ask ourselves whom we want to please. It's not always easy to choose modesty over style. It can be difficult to turn down a social opportunity that is contrary to God's design. But when we choose God, the satisfaction is more rewarding.

Dear God, I know You had my best interest at heart when You established Your standards. Help me to flee the temptation to water down Your Word for a mere moment of worldly pleasure.

Cultivating Contentment

I wait for the Lord. My soul waits and I hope in His Word.
My soul waits for the Lord more than one who watches for the
morning; yes, more than one who watches for the morning.

PSALM 130:5–6

What are you waiting for—a job, a relationship, physical healing, financial provision? Whatever answer to prayer you are longing for, remember that often it's in the waiting that God performs His perfecting work on our character. Joseph waited for many years, serving in Pharaoh's house (even ending up in jail) before God promoted Him. Abraham waited until he was a century old to see the child God had promised to him and Sarah decades before. God was still at work in both men's lives, though His actions and plans were hidden.

Maybe you've waited for God to come through, and so far, He hasn't. The word *advent* means "arrival or coming, especially one which is awaited." Like the silence the people of Israel endured for 400 years between the last spoken prophetic word and the arrival of the Christ child, perhaps you've endured silence from God for so long that you think He's not there, not listening—or not inclined to come to your rescue.

No matter what you're going through, please know that God is for you, not against you. He aches with you. And He offers us a choice: be chained in fear or changed by grace.

Which will you choose today?

Father, forgive me for doubting Your love and mercy.
Thank You that You are faithful and that You will
provide for me. I believe. . .help my unbelief.

The Perfect Redeemer

He said, "Who are you?" She answered, "I am Ruth, your woman servant. Spread your covering over me. For you are of our family."

RUTH 3:9

Ruth was a woman of faith. After suffering the loss of her husband, she could have wallowed in grief and misery. Instead, she chose to follow her mother-in-law, Naomi, to a place where she knew no one in order to honor her late husband (and, perhaps, the God he had introduced her to).

Ruth was also a woman of action. She worked hard to glean in the fields, toiling with intention and consistency. The owner of the fields, Boaz, noticed her work ethic and was impressed. Later, Ruth followed Naomi's advice and found Boaz at night while he was sleeping. Because he was a relative of hers and a man of integrity, he agreed to spread his covering over her as her "family redeemer." This meant he promised to marry and take care of Ruth (and Naomi).

Ruth's story has much to teach us. Just as Ruth moved on from grief to action, we can ask for God's help to move past our own losses and not get stuck in bitterness or anger. With His help, we can honor others and not wallow in self-pity or destructive habits. Also, as His strength and forgiveness cover our weaknesses and failures, we can find peace and joy. He is the perfect Redeemer who takes care of us so we don't have to worry about providing for ourselves.

My Rock and Redeemer, I praise and thank You for Your covering over me. You are a faithful provider.

A Promised Healing

*"See, I will make it well again, and I will heal them.
I will let them have much peace and truth."*

JEREMIAH 33:6

Are you longing to be healed of an affliction? Mary Magdalene suffered with seven demons before Jesus touched her and restored her to life. Scripture doesn't tell us much about how, when, or where Jesus healed Mary. It does tell us that Mary, along with several other women, provided for and supported Jesus so that He could do what God had called Him to do. After Jesus healed her, she became one of His most ardent followers.

This woman, who had been tormented by Satan himself, became a walking testimony of the power of the Light to dispel darkness: "The Light shines in the darkness. The darkness has never been able to put out the Light" (John 1:5).

Whether or not God chooses to cure you here on earth, one day He *will* resto"re you to total health. In heaven, our bodies will be perfect and no diseases will be allowed to touch us. We will live in peace and prosperity.

Such a promise should make us rejoice. Jesus will strengthen us for this life, whatever it may hold, and will one day turn on the light that will make the darkness scatter for all time. Hallelujah!

Heavenly Father, thank You for Your promise
of healing. Strengthen me as I walk this earth,
and give me hope as I look toward heaven.

Powered Up

God is able to do much more than we ask or think through His power working in us. May we see His shining-greatness in the church. May all people in all time honor Christ Jesus. Let it be so.

EPHESIANS 3:20–21

One day two blind men yelled out to Jesus. People tried to tell them to be quiet. But the men kept shouting, asking Him to have pity on them. Suddenly Jesus stopped in His tracks, then asked them, "What do you want Me to do for you?" (Matthew 20:32). The blind men said they wanted to see. And so, God honored that request. But the men got so much more in return. Not only did they obtain their vision, but they were also given the eye-opening opportunity to follow this Man of Miracles!

God is asking each of us the same question: "What do you want Me to do for you?" He wants us not to let others dissuade us from telling Him exactly what we want—no matter how impossible or improbable the request may seem. He wants us to be specific yet also to dream big—for He is a limitless God, ready to do so much more than we could ever ask or imagine! He wants us to then begin expecting the unexpected as we continue to travel with Him down the road with a lighter, more joyful step.

Lord, You have planted dreams within me. Power me up. Help me bring them to fruition beyond anything I could ever ask or imagine. To be specific, Lord, here's what I'd like. . . .

Firstfruits

Honor the Lord with your riches, and with the first of all you grow. Then your store-houses will be filled with many good things and your barrels will flow over with new wine.

PROVERBS 3:9–10

Perhaps you think this verse doesn't apply to you because you don't consider yourself *wealthy*. The only *produce* you have comes from the grocery store. *Store-houses* and *barrels of wine* may not be your top priority. But this verse applies. Read these words: *Honor the Lord. . .first of all.*

Our God is not a God of leftovers. He wants us to put Him first. One way to honor God is to give Him our "firstfruits," the best we have to offer. The truth is that everything we have comes from God. The Bible calls us to cheerfully give back to the Lord one-tenth of all we earn.

Giving to God has great reward. You may not have barns you need God to fill, but you will reap the benefit in other ways. When believers honor God by giving to Him, we can trust that He will provide for our needs. In Malachi 3:10, we are challenged to test God in our tithing. Start with your next paycheck. Make the check that you dedicate to God's kingdom work the first one you write. See if God is faithful to provide for you throughout the month.

Lord, remind me not to separate my finances from
my faith. All that I have comes from Your hand.
I will honor You with my firstfruits. Amen.

Feeling the Squeeze

The eye cannot say to the hand, "I do not need you."
Or the head cannot say to the feet, "I do not need you."
1 CORINTHIANS 12:21

We've all heard the term "the sandwich generation," referring to midlifers coping with teenagers on one end and aging parents on the other. Somehow, calling it a sandwich sounds too easy. The in-between filling seems to fit comfortably, like ham and swiss cheese nestled between two slices of rye bread. Sticking with the sandwich metaphor, a more appropriate term would be the "squeeze generation." Picture peanut butter and jelly oozing out of squished white bread. It is a challenging season of life.

So how do we keep our heads above water when every face we love is looking back at us with genuine, overwhelming needs? By learning to ask for help from family members, friends, the church, and even from resources available in the community.

It's a season in life when we need help. We can't do it alone. And perhaps that is a great blessing to realize. God never meant for us to do it alone! He designed us to live in community—family, friends, and church—helping and serving and meeting one another's needs. Paul told the believers at Corinth, "Our own body has many parts. When all these many parts are put together, they are only one body. The body of Christ is like this" (1 Corinthians 12:12).

There's nothing wrong with asking for help when you need it.

Lord, You promise never to leave us nor forsake us. Thank
You for providing helpers to come alongside of me. Amen.

More Than Words Can Say

"I will never leave you or let you be alone."

HEBREWS 13:5

Silence—for many people it can be quite uncomfortable. Televisions, stereos, and Spotify fill the void. Incessant conversation is the norm. Noise must permeate the air. What is it about silence that agitates us so? Perhaps pondering our own thoughts is frightening. Maybe we need constant reassurance from others that we are not alone.

We may desperately desire to hear from God, yet sometimes He chooses to remain silent. How do we interpret His silence? Do we become fearful, uneasy, or confused? We may feel that He has abandoned us, but this is not true. When God is silent, His love is still present. When God is silent, He is still in control. When God is silent, He is still communicating. Do not miss it. His silence speaks volumes.

Most couples who are deeply in love do not have to exchange words to communicate their love. They can experience contentment and unwavering trust in the midst of silence. The presence of their loved one is enough. That is what God desires in our love relationship with Him. He wants us to abide in His presence. Silence prohibits distraction. As we continue to trust Him amid the silence, we learn that His presence is all we need. God has promised that He will never leave us nor forsake us. Believe Him. Trust Him. His presence is enough.

Dear Lord, help me trust You even when You
choose to remain silent. May I learn how to
be content in Your presence alone. Amen.

Where Is Your Heart?

"For wherever your riches are, your heart will be there also."
MATTHEW 6:21

When others look at you, what kind of person do you want them to see? There may be many things you would wish to include in the list of adjectives that describe you. Maybe you aren't yet who you want to be, but you know you are a work in progress. Whatever the case, who you are is a very good indication of where your heart is.

For example, your attitude about your career is something people notice. Are you driven to succeed in order to obtain high position or salary? There's nothing wrong with desiring to succeed as long as you give God the glory and maintain a godly testimony. In fact, God could use a lot more God-fearing people running businesses and managing His finances.

If, however, you are willing to compromise God's standards in order to obtain position or wealth, your heart is not where it belongs. It is on corruptible things that will not last but that might destroy you if your attitude goes too far in the wrong direction.

Think about where your heart is in every decision you make. Ensure it is with those incorruptible things that matter. And as you direct your heart toward God, you will become the kind of person He wants you to be.

O Lord, give me wisdom to direct my heart
to lasting treasure that will honor You.

Humble Servant

Jesus knew the Father had put everything into His hands.
He knew He had come from God and was going back to God.
Jesus got up from the supper and took off His coat. He picked
up a cloth and put it around Him. Then He put water into
a wash pan and began to wash the feet of His followers. He
dried their feet with the cloth He had put around Himself.

JOHN 13:3–5

Imagine the twelve disciples in the upper room. Among them is the Son of God, with all authority given to Him by the Father. He has come to earth as a man and soon will return to heaven to sit at the Father's right hand. He puts a towel around His waist, pours water in a bowl, and kneels down before His disciples. He begins to wash feet—one of the lowliest jobs of that day. The Lord of the universe, the Living Word who speaks things into being and commands all things, makes a deliberate choice to get down on His knees and serve others. He handles their dusty feet, getting dirty Himself in order to make them clean. In word and deed, He teaches the disciples to follow His example. His humility is rooted in the quiet confidence of His relationship with His Father.

Are we willing to make a deliberate step to humble ourselves to serve others? Would we do the lowliest job? Will we enter into the messiness of each other's lives?

Lord, help me to follow Your example.
Make me a humble servant.

Heavenly Appreciation

God always does what is right. He will not forget the work
you did to help the Christians and the work you are still
doing to help them. This shows your love for Christ.

HEBREWS 6:10

Sometimes it seems our hard work is ignored. We sell a record number of lattes at the local coffee shop only to be told that we need to sell more pastries, or we spend days working on a presentation that the boss barely acknowledges. Our hard work seems unimportant, and we feel unappreciated.

Unfortunately, our work in the church can often feel the same way. We dutifully assume the role of greeter every Sunday, or we consistently fill communion cups each week. We spend each Sunday afternoon visiting the sick among the congregation, or we cook and serve weekly Wednesday night meals. Yet our work seems to go overlooked, and we wonder what the point is of our involvement in the church.

When our work for Christ seems to go unnoticed by our church family, we can be assured that God sees our hard work and appreciates it. We may not receive the "church member of the month" award, but our love for our brothers and sisters in Christ and our work on their behalf is not overlooked by God. The author of Hebrews assures us that God is not unjust—our reward is in heaven.

Dear Lord, You are a God of love and justice. Even
when I do not receive the notice of those around me,
help me to serve You out of my love for You. Amen.

Light in the Darkness

"I will lead the blind by a way that they do not know. I will lead them in paths they do not know. I will turn darkness into light in front of them. And I will make the bad places smooth."

ISAIAH 42:16

In the dim moonlight, we can sometimes find our way in the darkness of our homes. In familiar places, we know the lay of the land. At best, we will make our way around the obstacles through memory and shadowy outline. At worst, we will lightly stumble into an armchair or a piano bench. When all else fails, we know where the light switch is and, blindly groping in the darkness, we can turn on the light to help us find our way.

But when we walk in the darkness of unfamiliar places, we may feel unsettled. Not sure of our bearings, not knowing where the light switch is, we become overwhelmed, afraid to step forward, afraid even to move. At those times, we need to remember that our God of light is always with us. Although we may not see Him, we can rest easy, knowing He is ever-present in the darkness of unknown places, opportunities, and challenges.

God will never leave us to find our way alone. Realize this truth and arm yourself with the knowledge that no matter what the situation, no matter what the trial, no matter how black the darkness, He is ever there, reaching out for us, helping us find our way. Switch on the truth of His light in your mind, and walk forward, knowing He is always within reach.

Lord, be my Light. Guard me in the darkness of these days.
Make my way straight and the ground I trod smooth. And
if I do stumble, catch me! In Jesus' name, I pray. Amen.

Say You're Sorry

"Tear your heart and not your clothes." Return to the Lord your God.
JOEL 2:13

"Tell your sister you're sorry," Lynn instructed her younger daughter.

Blue eyes glaring, the four-year-old mumbled the ordered command. "Sorry."

How many times in a week do moms tell their children, "Say you're sorry"? And how many times does the "sorry" come out sounding like anything but an apology? There's sorrow for sin, and then there's sorrow for getting caught in sin. There's begrudging contrition, and then there's genuine repentance.

Pastor and Bible teacher David Jeremiah tells of unintentionally cutting off a woman in traffic. He could see she was angry. When he pulled into a fast-food drive-through, she was still behind him. So he did something she probably never expected. He paid for her order.

When God commands us to repent, He doesn't want a mumbled apology. He doesn't even want demonstrative tears—unless they come from a repentant heart. The scripture above from Joel shows true repentance. Repentance for sinning against God involves a willful action, a changing of direction. It's doing it God's way, going in God's direction. We can't always undo or fix all our wrong actions. But when it's in our power to do so, the Lord gives us specific guidelines. When we do our part, He does His because He "is full of loving-kindness" (Joel 2:13).

> Forgive me, Lord, for my sin against You and
> others. Help me to right those things I can right
> and not to repeat the same errors. Amen.

Too Busy for God?

"You can speak for Me," says the Lord. "You are My servant whom I have chosen so that you may know and believe Me, and understand that I am He. No God was made before Me, and there will be none after Me."

ISAIAH 43:10

Have you had thoughts like the following? *I am way too busy to spend time with the Lord today. I could have thirty more minutes today if I just skip my quiet time and get to work early.* Many of us feel uncomfortable admitting this, but how often do we skip our quiet time? How often do we think we are too busy to partake in fellowship with other believers one day a week? How often do we fail to participate in a Bible study because there is "homework" to complete?

When we are not engaging in the activities that draw us closer to the Lord, we are hindering ourselves from our true calling. God tells us that our purpose in life is to be His witnesses. We have been chosen to serve Him alone. God intends for us to be witnesses and to serve Him so that we may know and believe Him. God draws us into that intimate relationship of knowing Him through these Christian activities of quiet time, Bible study, and church attendance. As we deepen our relationship with the Lord, we will understand that we can trust and believe Him and then reflect Him to others through the many responsibilities He gives us.

Lord, thank You that I am chosen to serve as Your witness
in order to know and believe You. Particularly during busy
days, draw me into Your constant fellowship. Amen.

The Great Gift Giver

Whatever is good and perfect comes to us from God.
He is the One Who made all light. He does not
change. No shadow is made by His turning.

JAMES 1:17

Do you know a true gift giver? We all give gifts on birthdays and at Christmas, when we receive wedding invitations, and when a baby is born. But do you know someone with a real knack for gift giving? She finds all sorts of excuses for giving gifts. She delights in it. A true gift giver has an ability to locate that "something special." When shopping for a gift, she examines many items before making her selection. She knows the interests and preferences, the tastes and favorites of her friends and family members. She chooses gifts they will like—gifts that suit them well.

God is a gift giver. He is, in fact, the Creator of all good gifts. He finds great joy in blessing you. The God who made you certainly knows you by name. He knows your tastes and preferences. He even knows your favorites and your dreams. Most important, God knows your needs.

So in seasons of waiting in your life, rest assured that gifts chosen and presented to you by the hand of God will be worth the wait.

God, sometimes I am anxious. I want what I want,
and I want it now. Calm my spirit, and give me the
patience to wait for Your perfect gifts. Amen.

Troubled Bones

Be kind to me, O Lord, for I am weak. O Lord, heal me
for my bones are shaken. My soul is in great suffering.
But You, O Lord, how long?. . . The Lord has heard
my cry for help. The Lord receives my prayer.

PSALM 6:2–3, 9

We associate creaking, aching bones with aging, but they can strike at any age. Even children may suffer from rheumatoid arthritis; and sports injuries, cancer, and accidents do not spare the young.

We have not all broken a bone. But we do all know the deep-down pain of troubled bones. Illness and exhaustion carry physical pain. Broken relationships or the death of someone close to us weighs down our souls. Debts loom over us. Whatever the cause, we ache with a pain beyond words. Rest that refreshes the spirit as well as the body seems out of reach.

In the midst of that trouble, we wonder if God knows and hears us. With David, we cry, "How long? We can't take any more."

That cry is the starting point. God loves us, and the Holy Spirit carries our prayers to Him "with sounds that cannot be put into words" (Romans 8:26). God will answer every prayer at the right time according to His will.

The next time troubled bones keep us awake at night, we can take them to God in prayer.

Lord, our bones are troubled. We cry, "How long?"
We know You have heard our prayers. We ask that
You will give us peaceful rest in that assurance. Amen.

Forgiveness Hurts

"Forgive us our sins as we forgive those who sin against us."
MATTHEW 6:12

No one likes being wronged. Whether it's being cut off in traffic by a careless driver, gossiped about by a thoughtless friend, or hurt more deeply, we all have unresolved pain. A common feeling is to want the other person to experience the same pain we felt. Sometimes we follow through on our retaliation; other times no action is taken, but quiet festering and imagining take place in our minds. We want payback!

Unknown to us, the other person may not realize (or even care) that the wrong had such an effect on us. Sometimes we try to be the "bigger person" and resolve the issue. Other times that person might not want to address the issue, let alone claim any responsibility.

So what do we do? God says that we can do our part to examine the situation, acknowledge our responsibility, and attempt to move forward even if we don't receive an "I'm sorry." We may not forget the issue, but our stress, anxiety, and anger will be lessened because the issue will no longer be our focus. We will once again have the opportunity to live in and enjoy the present rather than concentrating on the past.

God chose to save us by sending His Son. The world reacted to this by abusing and killing Him. The next time hurt springs up, remember that God can especially relate to our feelings of being wronged.

Lord, thank You for forgiving my sins. Help me
to forgive and love others as You love me. Amen.

Lead Goose

Moses' father-in-law said to him, "What you are doing is not good. You and the people with you will become tired and weak. For the work is too much for you. You cannot do it alone."

EXODUS 18:17–18

The V formation of flying geese is a fascinating example of aerodynamics. Each bird flies slightly above the bird in front of it, resulting in a reduction of wind resistance. It also helps to conserve the goose's energy. The farther back a goose is in formation, the less energy it needs in the flight. The birds rotate the lead goose position, falling back when tired. With this instinctive system, geese can fly for a long time before they must stop for rest. This is an example of God's wisdom displayed in the natural world.

We often find ourselves as a lead goose. We have a hard time recognizing signs of exhaustion in ourselves. Even harder is falling back and letting someone else have a chance to develop leadership skills. Deep down we think that no other goose could get the gaggle where it needs to go without getting lost or bashing into treetops.

Jethro, Moses' father-in-law, came for a visit as the Israelites camped near the mountain of God. Jethro found Moses to be on the brink of exhaustion. "You will wear yourself out and these people as well," he told Moses. Jethro recommended that Moses delegate responsibilities. Moses listened and implemented everything Jethro suggested, advice that benefited the entire nation of Israel.

Dear Lord, help me to know when to fall back
and rest, letting someone else take the lead.
Teach me to serve You in any position. Amen.

Lay It at the Cross

"Come to Me, all of you who work and have heavy loads. I will give you rest. Follow My teachings and learn from Me. I am gentle and do not have pride. You will have rest for your souls. For My way of carrying a load is easy and My load is not heavy."

MATTHEW 11:28–30

Does life sometimes get you down? Often when we experience difficulties that weigh us down, we hear the old adage "Lay it at the cross." But how do we lay our difficulties at the cross?

Jesus gives us step-by-step guidance in how to place our difficulties and burdens at the foot of the cross. First, He invites us to come to Him; those of us who are weary and burdened just need to approach Jesus in prayer. Second, He exchanges our heavy and burdensome load with His easy and light load. Jesus gives us His yoke and encourages us to learn from Him. The word *yoke* refers to Christ's teachings, Jesus' *way* of living life. As we follow His teachings, we take his yoke in humility and gentleness, surrendering and submitting ourselves to His will and ways for our lives. Finally, we praise God for the rest He promises to provide us.

Do you have any difficulties in life, any burdens, worries, fears, relationship issues, finance troubles, or work problems that you need to "lay at the cross"? Jesus says, "Come."

Lord, thank You for inviting me to come and
exchange my heavy burden for Your light burden.
I praise You for the rest You promise me. Amen.

Keeping a Clean Heart

Since we have these great promises, dear friends, let us turn away from every sin of the body or of the spirit. Let us honor God with love and fear by giving ourselves to Him in every way.

2 CORINTHIANS 7:1

Her new home had white ceramic tile floors throughout. Upon seeing them, visiting friends and family often asked, "Won't they show every speck of dirt?"

"Yes, but at least I can tell if I need to clean them," replied the new homeowner, explaining her thinking that the better she could see the dirt, the better chance she had of keeping them sparkling clean.

"So how often do you have to clean them—once a week?" her friends asked.

"More like every day," she replied, laughing at their horrified faces.

Keeping a clean heart requires similar diligence and regular upkeep. While Jesus Himself cleanses us from all unrighteousness, as believers we need to be on the lookout for temptations and situations that might cause us to fall into sin in the first place. Reading the Bible reminds us that God is holy and that He expects us to strive for holiness in our thoughts and actions. As we pray daily, God shows us areas in our character or behaviors that are displeasing to Him and that need a thorough cleaning.

Like the homeowner who enjoyed knowing her floors were clean, there is joy and peace knowing our hearts can be clean too.

"Make a clean heart in me, O God. Give me a new spirit that will not be moved" [Psalm 51:10]. Amen.

Take Five

Then the Lord God made man from the dust of the ground. And He breathed into his nose the breath of life. Man became a living being.

GENESIS 2:7

How would you describe your physical and mental state today? Are you rested and refreshed, or do you feel weary, worn down by the unrelenting demands and pressures of doing life? We tend to think that the longer and harder we work, the more productive we will be. But when we become fatigued spiritually and emotionally, we eventually reach a point of exhaustion.

You *are* in control, and you *can* stop the world from spinning. Even if you know that it is impossible to take a day off, it helps tremendously to make time for a personal "time out."

Pause from whatever you are doing for just a few moments, and breathe deeply. Shut your office door, close your eyes, or pause for a second or two in the bathroom. Ask God for a sense of calm and clarity of mind to deal properly with your next responsibility. Take time to unwind from a stressful day by a few minutes of "me time" in the car as you drive home. If your commute is short, pull over for a few minutes and let the weight of the day fall off.

Sometimes the most active thing we can do is rest, even if for only a short time.

Father, help me not to push myself so hard.
Help me to remember to take five and breathe. Amen.

Creation's Praise

For You made the parts inside me.
You put me together inside my mother.
PSALM 139:13

God didn't spend seven days creating things and then put His creation abilities on the shelf. He is continually creating wonderful things for His people. He created each of us with a special design in mind. Nothing about us is hidden from Him—the good parts or the bad.

Before you had a thought or moved a muscle, God was working out a plan for your existence. Maybe He gave you brown hair and a sweet smile or good genes for a long life, or He gave you dark hair and clever fingers that are artistic. Perhaps He gave you a musical voice that worships Him daily in song. Whatever His gifts, He designed them just for you, to bring ministry to His hurting world.

When we look at the seven days of Creation, let's thank God that He didn't set things working and then walk away. Adam and Eve were important to Him, but so are we. He has personally created everything in this wonderful world—including us.

Do we need any more reason to praise the Lord who brought into existence every fiber of our beings?

Thank You, Lord, for detailing every piece of my body, mind, and spirit. I'm glad nothing that happens to me or in me is a surprise to You. Help me use all Your gifts to Your glory. Amen.

Reach Out and Touch

For she said to herself, "If I can only touch His coat, I will be healed."
MARK 5:28

We should never underestimate the power of touch. In our busy lives, as we rush from one appointment to another, skimping on affection with our families and loved ones can become routine. We wave good-bye to our children without stopping for a hug. Husbands head off to work with the barest brush of a kiss.

We do our loved ones a disservice, however, when we skip touching them. Touching communicates our affection but also our affirmation and sympathy. You can encourage people—or comfort them—with a simple touch. The Bible records Jesus touching many people, comforting and healing them. He also let people touch Him, such as the sinful woman who touched and kissed His feet (Luke 7:38).

In Mark 5, however, the true power of a simple touch is beautifully portrayed. This woman who had suffered for so long believed so strongly in Jesus that she knew the quickest touch of His hem would heal her. She reached out, and her faith made her well.

So hold those you love close. Hug them, and let them see a bit of Jesus' love in you every day.

Lord, I turn to You when I need comfort. Let me also
offer those around the comfort of a loving touch. Amen.

Behave Yourself!

I will be careful to live a life without blame. When will You come to me? I will walk within my house with a right and good heart.

PSALM 101:2

Home is where the heart is.

Home is a refuge, a place of rest.

Home is the smell of fresh-baked bread, the sound of laughter, the squeeze of a hug.

Because home is a place of comfort and relaxation, it is also the place where we are most likely to misbehave. We would never think of yelling at family members in public, for example, but if one of them pushes our buttons *just once* at home, we will instantly level her or him with a verbal machine gun.

David himself knew the danger of walking unwisely at home. He was home—not in battle—when he saw Bathsheba on the rooftop. His psalm cited above reminds us that we must behave wisely all the time, but especially at home.

Because more is caught than taught, our family must see mature behavior from us. We must model integrity—we must keep our promises and act the way we want those around us to act. Hypocrisy—"Do as I say, not as I do"—has no place in the home of a mature Christian who has been made complete in Christ.

May God grow us up into mature people, and may we walk accordingly, especially at home.

Father God, how often I fail at home. Make me sensitive to the Spirit so that I will recognize when I am straying from the path of maturity. I'm the adult here; help me to act as one. Amen.

Difficult People

*Christian brother, you were chosen to be free. Be careful that
you do not please your old selves by sinning because you are
free. Live this free life by loving and helping others.*

GALATIANS 5:13

In the classic movie *An Affair to Remember*, Deborah Kerr asks Cary Grant,
"What makes life so difficult?" to which he responds, "People?"

Yes, people tend to make our lives difficult. But they also make life
worth living. The trick is not to let the biting words or nefarious deeds
of others become glaring giants that make us flee or weigh us down with
hate and resentment.

The only way David stood up to the giant Goliath was by turning his
problem over to the Lord and relying on His strength and power. Then,
acting in faith, David prevailed with the weapons at hand—a slingshot
and one smooth stone.

Sometimes, like David, we need to turn our skirmishes with others over
to the Lord. Then, by using our weapons—God's Word and a steadfast
faith—we need to love and forgive others as God loves and forgives us.

Always keep in mind that, although we may not like to admit it, we
have all said and done some pretty awful things ourselves, making the
lives of others difficult. Yet God has forgiven us *and* continues to love us.

So do the right thing. Pull your feet out of the mire of unforgive-
ness, sidestep verbal retaliation, and stand tall in the freedom of love
and forgiveness.

The words and deeds of others have left me wounded and
bleeding. Forgiveness and love seem to be the last thing
on my mind. Change my heart, Lord. Help me to love and
forgive others as You love and forgive me. Amen.

Take Time to Take Time

Remember how fast my life is passing.

PSALM 89:47

You stroll a sandy, white beach as a warm breeze sweeps across your face. Broken waves froth against your bare feet and seagulls soar above. You breathe in the fresh sea air. . .and then reality interrupts the daydream.

"Time and tide wait for no man," reads one quote. As surely as the tide rises and falls, time passes swiftly. Like a wet bar of soap slipping through our fisted hand, we lose grip on time as good intentions fall prey to crowded schedules. Our busy pace deters us from taking a walk on the beach, having lunch with a friend, or making a date with our significant other.

King David recognized the brevity of life when viewed through the window of eternity. Often we fool ourselves into thinking that we have plenty of time; meanwhile, months and years pass by seemingly without notice.

Is time passing you by? Have you allowed other things to rob you of much-needed time apart? It's never too late to grab a new bar of soap, cling loosely, and take that much-deserved walk on the beach.

Dear Lord, time flies, and I've let it pass me by. I want to use the time You've given me more effectively. I want to enjoy life. Help me to take time out for myself and for others. Amen.

Lost and Found

*"He that sent Me is with Me. The Father has not left
Me alone. I always do what He wants Me to do."*

JOHN 8:29

We lose things on a daily basis. Each year we probably spend hours looking for things—keys, sunglasses, lipstick, or even the saltshaker that normally rests next to the stove. We know these items don't sprout wings and walk off but have been set somewhere and forgotten by you or someone you know.

You are God's most prized possession, and while He'll never forget where you are, sometimes we walk off from Him. We lose ourselves in the things we need to do, the places we need to go, and the people we need to see. Our calendars fill up with commitments we're obligated to keep. We often commit to too many things and exhaust ourselves trying to stay ahead of our schedules.

The further we displace ourselves from God—not necessarily on purpose—the more we become lost in our own space. While we're doing life on our own, we can forget that He is standing there waiting to do life every day with us. If you feel distant from Him today, look up. He's waiting for you to find your rightful place with Him.

God, I never want to become so busy that I lose sight of You.
Show me what things I should commit to and what things
are for someone else to do so that I am available to You and
ready to serve in the capacity You've prepared me for. Amen.

The Practice of Praise

Praise the Lord, O my soul. And all that is within me, praise His holy name. Praise the Lord, O my soul. And forget none of His acts of kindness. He forgives all my sins. He heals all my diseases. He saves my life from the grave. He crowns me with loving-kindness and pity.

PSALM 103:1–4

Trials come to all of us, and when they do, it's easy to forget all that God has done for us in the past. Often our adverse circumstances sabotage our efforts to praise God in every situation.

The psalmist practiced the power of praise as he acknowledged God's faithfulness to forgive, heal, and restore. He blessed the Lord with his whole heart because he trusted in God's divine plan.

Positive acclamations of our faith produce remarkable results. First, praise establishes and builds our faith. It decrees, "No matter what is happening, no matter how I feel, I choose to praise God!" Second, praise changes our perspective. As we relinquish control, praise redirects our focus toward God rather than on our problems. And third, praise blesses the heart of God. It brings God joy for His children to acknowledge His presence and power through praise.

The Bible admonishes us to praise God in every circumstance, saying, "In everything give thanks. This is what God wants you to do because of Christ Jesus" (1 Thessalonians 5:18). To bless the Lord in all things is to receive God's blessings. Begin the practice of praise today!

Heavenly Father, You are worthy of all my praise. I thank and praise You for my current circumstances, knowing that You are at work on my behalf. Amen.

Changing Direction

Then God spoke to them in a dream. He told them not to go back
to Herod. So they went to their own country by another road.
MATTHEW 2:12

Wise men, having seen a shining star in the east, headed to Jerusalem, where they asked King Herod about the birth of the King of the Jews. Herod, a cruel and crafty tyrant, sent the wise men to Bethlehem, telling them to search for this Child and, after finding Him, to come back and bring him word.

So the wise men left Herod, continued to follow the star, and eventually were led to Jesus' house, where they presented Him with their gifts. Then, being warned by God in a dream not to go back to Herod, they returned home by another way.

Do *we* listen to God that well? Are we able to change direction at God's prompting? Or are we bent on following the route we have set before us and then are somehow surprised when we come face-to-face with a Herod?

We would do best to become wise, daily presenting ourselves to Jesus, asking Him to lead us on the right path, and keeping a weather eye on the heavenly sky. Then, alert for God's directional promptings, we will avoid the Herods of this world.

By following God's direction—in a dream, His Word, your quiet time, or conversations with others—you will be sure to stay on the right path and arrive home safely.

Jesus, I present myself to You. Show me the right
path to walk with every step I take. Keep me away
from evil, and lead me to Your door. Amen.

Nothing to Lose

Saul said to David, "You are not able to go and fight against this Philistine. You are only a young man, while he has been a man of war since he was young."

1 SAMUEL 17:33

Goliath, a pagan Philistine, defied Israel's army and challenged it to send a single man to fight him to decide who would rule the land. As the Israelites observed his giant body and fearsome war equipment, they quaked in their sandals. How could they win?

Victory lay in the hands of a visionary shepherd, David, who recognized that the battle was not his but God's. The intrepid shepherd stepped forward to accept the challenge.

"Wiser" heads warned the youth of danger. King Saul counseled against fighting the Philistine warrior, then tried to deck the shepherd out in his own armor. But David had a better armor—the Lord God.

Sometimes we clearly hear the call of God to move ahead into spiritual battle. Others warn us against it, and their counsel seems wise. But God's call pulls at our hearts. Who are we listening to? Are these counselors godly people or discouraging, worldly wise Sauls, with at best a tenuous connection to God?

If God is fighting your battle for you, trust in Him, seek godly counsel, and follow His call implicitly. You have nothing to lose.

If You lead me, Lord, I cannot lose. Show me
Your path and give me courage. Amen.

Follow Your Heart

*"I was forty years old when the Lord's servant Moses sent
me from Kadesh-barnea to spy out the land. I returned
with news for him as it was in my heart."*

JOSHUA 14:7

Sometimes when we speak our hearts, we come against opposition. This is
nothing new. The same thing happened to Caleb when he and the other
Israelites were sent to spy out the land of Canaan. When the spies came
back to Moses and the people, everyone but Joshua and Caleb gave a
bad report. Those driven by fear said there was no way Israel could take
possession of the land. The current tenants—giants, to be exact—were too
strong for God's people to overcome.

Yet Caleb and Joshua, the men whose spirits witnessed with God's
Spirit, knew the truth of the matter. They alone stood against the bearers
of bad report. They spoke the truth in their hearts—truth that was met
by the tears and mourning of the Israelites who feared the giants, were
disgusted with their leaders, and rejected God.

Don't let naysayers mislead you. Walk uprightly, and speak the truth
in your heart (see Psalm 15:2). Although the going may get rough—with
giants and unbelievers obstructing your path—by following your heart
and God, you will never lose your way on your journey to the land of
milk and honey.

God, give me the courage to speak from my heart. Stand
beside me, lead me in the right direction, and grant me Your
wisdom as I step out from among the crowd. Amen.

In the Light

Jesus spoke to all the people, saying, "I am the Light of the world. Anyone who follows Me will not walk in darkness. He will have the Light of Life."

JOHN 8:12

The hurricane forced the family to huddle inside without electricity for a second consecutive day. If days were dreary, nights seemed eternal. Not knowing how long they would be without electricity, they conserved flashlight batteries, candles, and oil for the lamp. Even walking posed a challenge without tripping over the dog or whacking a chair leg. Games and conversation by candlelight soon lost their appeal. Reading strained the eyes. By eight o'clock there was nothing else to do but go to bed and sweat for hours on end, praying for sunshine the next morning.

The basics of life were difficult and burdensome. When the dark clouds finally lifted, sunlight streamed in and power was restored. Despite the mess outside, their spirits were revived.

Jesus said followers will never have to walk in darkness again but will have a life in the light. No more stumbling—we have His guidance. No more dreariness—we have His joy. No more heaviness—we have freedom to bask in the warmth of His forgiveness! His light of life is a vibrant life lived confidently because we can see the path before us through eyes of faith.

Light of Life, thank You that we do not hover in darkness any longer. In You we walk boldly in the light of life, forgiven, free, and vibrant. Amen.

Comfort Food

*Everything that was written in the Holy Writings
long ago was written to teach us. By not giving up,
God's Word gives us strength and hope.*

ROMANS 15:4

A big mound of ice cream topped with hot fudge; a full bowl of salty, buttery popcorn; grilled cheese sandwiches and warm chicken noodle soup fixed by Mom—comfort food. There is nothing like a generous helping of things that bring the sensation of comfort to a worn body at the end of a long day or to a bruised mind after a disappointment. Those comfort foods soothe the body and mind because, through the senses, they remind us of happier and more secure times.

Romans 15:4 tells us that the scriptures are comfort food for the soul. They were written and given so that, through our learning, we would be comforted with the truths of God. Worldly pleasures bring a temporary comfort, but the problem still remains when the pleasure or comfort fades. However, the words of God are soothing and provide permanent hope and peace. Through God's Word, you will be changed, and your troubles will dim in the bright light of Christ. So the next time you are sad, lonely, or disappointed, before you turn to pizza, turn to the Word of God as your source of comfort.

Thank You, Father, for the rich comfort Your Word provides.
Help me to remember to find my comfort in scripture rather
than through earthly things that will ultimately fail me. Amen.

A Pure Heart

Keep your heart pure for out of it are the important things of life.
PROVERBS 4:23

Do the words of Proverbs 4:23 instruct us to isolate ourselves, building walls around our hearts like fortresses to keep others out? Should we avoid letting others touch our lives and get close to us? Certainly this is not what God would want! We are designed for fellowship with other believers and even for an intimate, loving relationship with a spouse. Guarding our hearts, however, is an important command that many people in the twenty-first century often fail to heed.

When we fall into relationships or activities that are unhealthy or that consume us, our hearts lose their focus and get wounded along the way. Even good things can become idols in our lives. An idol is anything that we allow to come before God. The Lord is always there to take us back and to help us heal, but He would much prefer to help us make wise decisions on the front end. If we seek God first in all things, He can protect us from pitfalls.

Christians are meant for a close walk with God, talking with Him daily, reading and applying His Word. This walk suffers when our hearts are given carelessly to other things or people in our lives. We must, therefore, *keep our hearts pure* in order that we may live the abundant lives God desires for us.

Father, help me to love freely but also to guard my heart. Walk and talk with me today. Guide the steps that I take. Amen.

I Have Arrived

"Who knows if you have not become queen for such a time as this?"

ESTHER 4:14

You may have experienced a time in your life when you thought, *I'm precisely where God destined me to be at this point in my life.* Did you feel as if you had arrived—or that you had found the very thing you were created to do?

Maybe you felt complete after the first week at a new job. Perhaps you found your niche in volunteering at church or for a worthy organization. In that season, God equipped you to fulfill your purpose, but even greater moments are awaiting you.

There is coming a day in which each one of us will truly be able to say, "I have arrived!" When we reach heaven and are able to worship God face-to-face, then we will be able to say that we are doing what we were destined to do—worship the very One who created us.

Then we will look around and say, "I have arrived!"

Heavenly Father, thank You for giving me a dream and a destiny. I want to serve You in the very purpose You created me for—today and into all of eternity. Amen.

Location, Location, Location

He who lives in the safe place of the Most High will be in the shadow of the All-powerful. I will say to the Lord, "You are my safe and strong place, my God, in Whom I trust."

PSALM 91:1–2

Where do you live? Where are you living right now, this instant?

If you are abiding in Christ, moment by moment, you are constantly safe under His protection. In that secret place, that hidden place in Him, you can maintain a holy serenity, a peace of mind that surpasses all understanding. If you are trusting in God, nothing can move you or harm you.

If money problems, physical illness, time pressures, job woes, the state of the world, or something else is getting you down, check your location. Where are you? Where is your mind? Where are your thoughts?

Let what the world has conditioned you to think go in one ear and out the other. Stand on the truth, the promises of God's Word. Say of the Lord, "God is my refuge! I am hidden in Christ! Nothing can harm me. In Him I trust!" Say it loud. Say it often. Say it over and over until it becomes your reality. And you will find yourself dwelling in that secret place every moment of the day.

God, You are my refuge. When I abide in You, nothing can harm me. Your Word is the truth on which I rely. Fill me with Your light and the peace of Your love. It's You and me, Lord, all the way! Amen.

Reality Check

Your heart should be holy and set apart for the Lord God. Always be ready to tell everyone who asks you why you believe as you do. Be gentle as you speak and show respect. Keep your heart telling you that you have done what is right. If men speak against you, they will be ashamed when they see the good way you have lived as a Christian.

1 Peter 3:15–16

Researchers sometimes conduct behavioral studies on groups of people. The hope is often to observe the similarities and differences in individuals' character, attitude, and behavior and learn from them.

To make the study effective, subjects are not always told they are being watched but instead think they are simply in a holding room, waiting for the study to begin. The study's conductors often are watching and listening from behind mirrors or walls.

Findings show that people's speech and attitudes often are different in public than they are in private. When in public, people seem to put on faces and attitudes that don't reflect their real selves.

Every day we are being watched—both by the Father and by the people around us. Our attitudes and speech often are weighed against beliefs we profess and the hope we claim. Take time to search your heart and your motivations. If your speech and attitude aren't Christ-centered, re-aim your heart to hit the mark.

Lord, help me to be a good representative for You. Amen.

Board God's Boat

He said to them, "Come away from the people. Be by yourselves and rest." There were many people coming and going. They had had no time even to eat.

MARK 6:31

Are you "missing the boat" to a quieter place of rest with God? You mean to slow down, but your church, work, and family responsibilities pile higher than a stack of recyclable newspapers. Just when you think a free moment is yours, the phone rings, a needy friend stops by, or your child announces she needs you to bake cookies for tomorrow's school fund-raiser.

The apostles ministered tirelessly—so much so, they had little time to eat. As they gathered around Jesus to report their activities, the Lord noticed that they had neglected to take time for themselves. Sensitive to their needs, the Savior instructed them to retreat by boat with Him to a solitary place of rest where He was able to minister to them.

Often we allow the hectic pace of daily life to drain us physically and spiritually, and in the process, we deny ourselves time alone to pray and read God's Word. Meanwhile, God patiently waits.

So perhaps it's time to board God's boat to a quieter place and not jump ship!

Heavenly Father, in my hectic life, I've neglected time apart with You. Help me to board Your boat and stay afloat through spending time in Your Word and in prayer. Amen.

Choosing What Your Life Looks Like

All those who are led by the Holy Spirit are sons of God.
ROMANS 8:14

"He's Got the Whole World in His Hands" is a song that generations of children have sung for years. The lyrics of this song say that God is in control and that whatever is going to happen in our lives will happen no matter what.

The truth is, you were created in God's image with a will, and that means you have the right to choose your own life, whether it's what God desires most for you or not.

Jesus said, "Not my will, but Yours, Father!" He chose to live God's dream for His life over His own. Each day you also decide what your life looks like. The Spirit of God stands ready to lead and guide you, but you must choose to follow His lead to reach the destiny He planned for you.

He has the whole world in His hands, but daily choices belong to you. Choose to live in His will, making decisions based on His direction. Knowing His will comes from a personal relationship and from time spent with Him in prayer and in the Word. Jesus knew the path laid before Him, and you can too. Choose today.

Heavenly Father, thank You for making a way to form me to be Your child. I choose Your dream, Your destiny for my life. Help me to make the right choices for my life as I follow You. Amen.

162

Be Strong and Courageous

"Have I not told you? Be strong and have strength of heart! Do not be afraid or lose faith. For the Lord your God is with you anywhere you go."

JOSHUA 1:9

In Joshua 1:9, God demands Joshua to "be strong and have strength of heart," a phrase that is repeated five more times in the book of Joshua. When God repeatedly demands something, we would do well to pay attention. But are we listening to God, or are we letting the fears of this world paralyze us?

Many things in this world can terrify us—the state of the economy, terrorist threats, the current crime rate, another car swerving into our lane of traffic—the list goes on and on. But we are to take courage and be strong. We are *commanded* to do so.

Someone has calculated that the words *fear not* appear exactly 365 times in the Bible. How wonderful to have this affirmation available to us every day of the year! Praise God that with Christ the Deliverer in our lives, we are no longer threatened by the world around us. He has overcome all! Now all *we* need to do is believe it!

Believe that God is with you every moment of the day. Believe that He has the power to protect and shield you from the poisonous darts of the evil one. Believe that He has overcome the world. Believe that with Him by your side, you can be stronger than the world's most powerful army. Believe that you have the courage to face the unfaceable. Nothing on this earth can harm you.

Today, Lord, I will not fear. No matter what comes
against me, I am strong and courageous, able to overcome
any foe—because You are by my side! Amen.

God's Joy

Ezra said to them, "Go, eat and drink what you enjoy, and give
some to him who has nothing ready. For this day is holy to our
Lord. Do not be sad for the joy of the Lord is your strength."
NEHEMIAH 8:10

The beginning of each month brings a daunting mound of things to accomplish. However, looking back to God's provision during the past month gives His children hope. Nehemiah encouraged the Israelites after they finished rebuilding the walls of Jerusalem to enjoy themselves (in a godly manner). They endured scorn, weariness, and threats from the nations around them as they were rebuilding their homes, but God protected them and blessed their work. When they were tempted to wallow in regret over past wrongs, they were told not to be burdened by guilt but to go forward doing what is pleasing and joyous to God. God's joy is in the faith of His children, and staying close to God is what gives His creation joy and strength no matter what may come in the future. The Israelites were also told to give to those in need as part of their celebration so that everyone could share in the joy. The passage says that when the people understood what they were told—God's message of hope—they rejoiced greatly. This month is another opportunity to repent of wrong-doings and enjoy the Father's ever-present goodness.

Father God, thank You for the redemption hope You
give through Jesus. Help us to leave the burdens of
the past and the worries of the future in Your hands.
In Your joy we find true joy and lasting strength.

He Chose

"The Lord did not give you His love and choose you because you were more people than any of the nations. For the number of your people was less than all nations. But it is because the Lord loves you and is keeping the promise He made to your fathers."

DEUTERONOMY 7:7–8

In the book of Deuteronomy, God tells the people of Israel that they are unique. Who else has "heard the voice of God speaking out of the midst of the fire" and lived? What other nation could claim that Jehovah was on their side as they saw all the miracles God did for them? However, God says that this special treatment, this unique relationship with the one true God, is not a result of anything done by the Israelites. They did nothing to deserve this love; it was freely given to them. They were actually a terribly rebellious and ungrateful people. However, God still reached down to them and constantly assured them of His love and presence. Many people today seek to do things to gain acceptance or affection. They judge their worth by their accomplishments, looks, possessions. But God says He loves His people, and it is nothing they do which makes them right with God. It is only God's grace, evidenced most powerfully through the death and resurrection of Jesus, that produces the Maker's love. He chose to love and to save. What's more, He chose to love the least.

Father, humble us when we think we can reach You
by our own strength. When we are discouraged and
weary, let us remember that You love us still.

Comfort in Sadness

You have seen how many places I have gone. Put my
tears in Your bottle. Are they not in Your book?

PSALM 56:8

In heaven there will be no more sadness. Tears will be a thing of the past. For now, we live in a fallen world. There are heartaches and disappointments. Some of us are more prone to crying than others, but all of us have cause to weep at times.

Call out to God when you find yourself tossing and turning at night or when tears drench your pillow. He is a God who sees, a God who knows. He is your "Abba" Father, your daddy.

It hurts the Father's heart when you cry, but He sees the big picture. God knows that gut-wrenching trials create perseverance in His beloved child and that perseverance results in strong character.

Do you ever wonder if God has forgotten you and left you to fend for yourself? Rest assured that He has not left you even for one moment. He is your Good Shepherd, and you are His lamb. When you go astray, He spends every day and every night calling after you. If you are a believer, then you know your Good Shepherd's voice.

*Shhhh...listen...*He is whispering a message of comfort even now.

Father, remind me that You are a God who sees my pain.
Jesus, I thank You that You gave up Your life for me. Holy
Spirit, comfort me in my times of deep sadness. Amen.

Be Still

"You will keep the man in perfect peace whose
mind is kept on You, because he trusts in You."
ISAIAH 26:3

If you watch the news on a regular basis, you'll find that our world is full of chaos and despair. And while most newscasts only focus on bad news, there's no denying that much of the world is in turmoil. Hurricanes, terrorism, school shootings—it's enough to make hibernation an attractive option.

During the prophet Isaiah's time, the Israelites faced their own reasons for discouragement and fear. They had been taken from their homes, forced into captivity, and persecuted for their faith. And although much of their suffering stemmed from their disobedience to God, He had compassion on them. Longing for His children to know His peace, God sent prophets like Isaiah to stir up faith, repentance, and comfort in the hearts of the "chosen people." God's message is just as applicable today as it was back then. By keeping our minds fixed on Him, we can have perfect, abiding peace even in the midst of a crazy world. The path to peace is not easy, but it is simple: focus on God. As we meditate on His promises and His faithfulness, He gets bigger, while our problems get smaller.

God, when I focus on the world, my mind and
heart feel anxious. Help me to keep my mind
on You so that I can have hope and peace.

I Am

And God said to Moses, "I AM WHO I AM." And He said,
"Say to the Israelites, 'I AM has sent me to you.'"

EXODUS 3:14

The words "I am" ring out in the present tense. These words are used some seven hundred times in the Bible to describe God and Jesus. When Moses was on the mount and asked God who He was, a voice thundered, "I Am." In the New Testament, Jesus said of Himself, "I am the bread of life; I am the light of the world; I am the Good Shepherd; I am the way; I am the resurrection." Present tense. Words of hope and life. I Am.

Who is God to you today? Is He in the present tense? Living, loving, presiding over your life? Is the Lord of Lords "I Was" or "I've Never Been" to you? Have you experienced the hope that comes from an everlasting "I Am" Father? One who walks by you daily and will never let go? "I Am with you always."

We are surprised when we struggle in the world, yet we hesitate to turn to our very Creator. He has the answers, and He will fill you with hope. Reach for Him today. Don't be uncertain. Know Him. For He is, after all, I Am.

Father, we surrender our lives to You this day. We choose
to turn from our sins, reach for Your hand, and ask for Your
guidance. Thank You for Your loving-kindness. Amen.

Thank You

But as for me, I will always have hope and I will praise You more and
more. My mouth will tell about how right and good You are and about
Your saving acts all day long. For there are more than I can know.

PSALM 71:14–15

Those in the workplace, be it an office or at home, really appreciate a
"thanks—well done" every now and then. Kudos can make the day go
smoother. And when others brag on us a tad, it perks up the attitude.
Think then how our heavenly Father loves to hear a hearty "thank You"
from His kids.

Our lives should be filled with praise to the Living Lord and King of
kings. He is a mighty God who created us and watches over us. We ought
to tell others of the deeds He has done in our lives for the power of our
testimony is great. Tell how He is our Savior and our hope. The psalmist
exhorts us to hope continually because we know even in the darkest days,
He has given us a promise to never leave our sides.

Synonyms for praise include *admire, extol, honor, glorify, honor,* and
worship. This day take one or two of these words and use them to thank
your heavenly Father. Don't take Him for granted. Give Him the praise
He deserves.

Father God, how good You are. You have blessed us immeasurably,
and for that we choose to glorify Your name. Let us shout it
from the mountain: our God is good, forever and ever. Amen.

Strength

Then Hannah prayed and said, "My heart is happy in the Lord. My strength is honored in the Lord. My mouth speaks with strength against those who hate me, because I have joy in Your saving power. There is no one holy like the Lord. For sure, there is no one other than You. There is no rock like our God."

1 SAMUEL 2:1–2

Hannah was filled with sorrow because she could not have children, and her husband's other wife taunted her because of this. Even though Hannah was the favorite wife (her name means favored), she still longed to be a mother. So she brought her suffering heart before God in prayer, and God graciously answered. He gave her a son whom she named Samuel and who became one of the greatest judges and prophets of the Old Testament. God did not stop there. He also gave her five other children after Samuel. Hannah acknowledges that Jehovah God is her strength. In her deepest pain and overwhelming despair, she first turned to God. His answer filled the longing in her heart and drew her to a deeper worship of God. He is the only one who can give strength to overcome the worries of this world. God calls His children to seek deliverance from their burdens only in Him because any other option is futile and fleeting.

Rock of Ages, help Your children to rejoice in You as their strength. Keep us from trusting in ourselves, and remind us that You answer prayers often in unexpected ways.

Written on Him

"Can a woman forget her nursing child? Can she have no pity on the son to whom she gave birth? Even these may forget, but I will not forget you. See, I have marked your names on My hands. Your walls are always before Me."

ISAIAH 49:15–16

God's people, during the life of the prophet Isaiah, were under threat of captivity, and they saw impending doom. They knew their dark and rebellious hearts brought this about, and they feared that Jehovah would forget or forsake them. God responded by likening Himself to a mother—the ultimate symbol of love and devotion. Mothers care for their children to guide and protect them. However, in this fallen world, there are also women who abandon their children. God says that unlike weak and broken earthly parents, He will remain steadfast. He can do no less when He says that He marked His children on the palms of His hands. Carved into His hands! This image comes to life when Jesus took nails through His hands to save sinners and make them children of God. What a powerful promise: He will never leave us nor forsake us.

Holy God, thank You that we can call You Abba, or Daddy. Thank You that Jesus suffered, died, and rose again so that people of all tribes and nations could know You as Father. Thank You that You never forget Your children. Help us to never doubt Your compassion, provision, and love.

Free at Last

The heart is free where the Spirit of the
Lord is. The Lord is the Spirit.
2 CORINTHIANS 3:17

Rules exist to keep order in our lives and to establish boundaries. Parents have rules for their children; the police have rules for drivers. All are necessary for humans to get along with each other, to cooperate. And when people operate completely outside of the rules, chaos can ensue. So when we begin life as a Christian, we learn that Jesus did not come to bring chaos—He came to bring each of us a new life.

In scripture, Paul was speaking to the church in Corinth, but he certainly wasn't telling them to throw caution to the wind and live completely outside the box. What he was saying was once the Spirit of the Living God lives inside you, there is freedom, an emancipation from bondage, a release from sin. What a cause for rejoicing! Free indeed.

But we cannot live this way in our own power. When we form this covenant with God and are saved, then with Jesus and the Holy Spirit, we can defeat the enemy who is trying to steal and destroy. Put on this armor to face the world. Be ready for the fight. Look to the Word to provide you with the needed tools to walk through each day.

Father God, thank You for the Holy Spirit that You have placed
inside my heart. Quicken me to hear Your voice. Amen.

Cleaning Up

Come close to God and He will come close to you. Wash your hands, you sinners. Clean up your hearts, you who want to follow the sinful ways of the world and God at the same time.

JAMES 4:8

Picture a muddy, unshorn sheep. A shepherd would have a job before him to clean up that animal because the fleece is quite deep. He must dig down with the shears layer by layer, tugging at the wool as he goes. In order to shear the sheep, he has to have hold of it, a firm grasp on a wiggling, uncooperative animal. Whatever it takes, the shepherd cleans the sheep.

Now picture us. Uncooperative, squirming, with insides that need to be cleaned. Our thoughts and actions have not been pure. Maybe we have lost our temper, taken advantage of another, or gossiped. Actions that are not what God wants of us. Actions that are called sin. Sin that blackens the heart. Like the sheep, we must be gathered in and cleaned.

Our most glorious God has promised He will do that for us when we ask. If we draw near to God and ask for His forgiveness, He will cleanse our hearts and make us part of His fold. Hallelujah. What a magnificent and overwhelming plan He has for us!

Dear Lord, is gaining a new life truly as simple as that? I reach out my hand in surrender and ask You to become the King of my life. Thank You for all You have done for me. Amen.

Life in the Light

Of what great worth is Your loving-kindness, O God! The children of men come and are safe in the shadow of Your wings. They are filled with the riches of Your house. And You give them a drink from Your river of joy. All life came from You. In Your light we see light.

PSALM 36:7–9

David packs so many beautiful metaphors in the verses above that reveal to readers important aspects of God's character.

His love is unfailing, and no price could ever be put on this love.

People find comfort and protection when they turn to God's love and when they seek to do everything according to God's will—this is what it means to be in the shadow of His presence.

It is in the presence of God that people have a veritable feast for the soul, which is evidenced materially or physically. God fills the spiritual thirst of people by giving them of Himself—knowledge of Himself, instilling in them His love, and giving them His characteristics.

Just as Jesus preached in the Sermon on the Mount in Matthew, chapter five (where he also provided physical bread), God will bless and fill those who hunger for and thirst after the goodness and purity of God. The Creator God is the source of all life, and it is only through Him that humans can understand the meaning and purpose of existence. It is His Light—Christ—that gives us life.

Great Refuge, illuminate our minds and hearts to see
the light that is Christ and to be beacons from which
this light shines onto others who are in darkness.

Fragrant Prayers

May my prayer be like special perfume before You. May the lifting up of my hands be like the evening gift given on the altar in worship.

PSALM 141:2

Coming before God in honest prayer is often difficult. There are many distractions offered by the world. Prayer is also easily corrupted into something it should not be, which is why Jesus spends so much time emphasizing the need to dispel previous conceptions of prayer. He presents prayer as a very personal and intimate conversation with the Father. The Bible is filled with examples of the importance of heartfelt and sincere prayers. God asks His children to bring Him something beautiful in their prayers; and if His children love Him, then they long to give Him sweet-smelling prayers. What makes prayers beautiful? Throughout the Bible, God reveals that prayers should be a mixture of praise, confession of sins, and petitions. The humble heart of the one praying, who lets the Holy Spirit work in them, makes the most beautiful of prayers. It is not the use of clever words that draws God's ear, but words that show a desire to know Him at a deeper level. When His children pray with their whole being, the position of the heart, mind, and body are all affected. The beautiful fragrance of Christ will follow His children wherever they go.

Father, we echo the voice of the psalmist in saying that we want our prayers to be drenched in Your Word and to be like sweet-smelling incense before You. Let us continue both day and night to fellowship with You in prayer.

Experience Anew the
Beautiful Wisdom of God's Word

THE REFRESHINGLY APPROACHABLE
NEW LIFE VERSION OF THE BIBLE

The Bible can change your life—and the New Life™ Version
makes scripture easier than ever to understand. Based on a limited
vocabulary of approximately 1,200 words, the NLV clarifies
difficult words and passages for better understanding.
Looking for a fresh perspective on God's Word?
These lovely Bibles are for you!

Hardback–Printed Cloth / $29.99

More Beautiful Wisdom Resources for Your Lovely Spirit

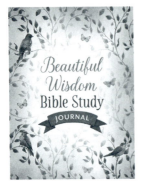

BEAUTIFUL WISDOM BIBLE STUDY JOURNAL

Providing encouraging, edifying quotations, New Life Version scriptures, and ample space for users to record your insights, this beautiful journal can become a treasured keepsake of your spiritual journey.

Flexible Casebound / 978-1-63609-273-7 / $19.99

THE BEAUTIFUL WISDOM BIBLE PROMISE BOOK

With nearly 1,000 Bible verses, this book features scripture in the easy-to-understand New Life Bible arranged in categories like Adversity, Duty, Friendship, Modesty, Protection, Sincerity, Strength, and Zeal.

Flexible Casebound / 978-1-63609-294-2 / $12.99

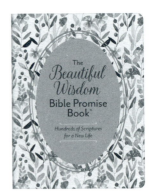